THE FUTURE OF TURKISH DEMOCRACY

HEARING

BEFORE THE

SUBCOMMITTEE ON EUROPE, EURASIA, AND EMERGING THREATS

OF THE

COMMITTEE ON FOREIGN AFFAIRS
HOUSE OF REPRESENTATIVES

ONE HUNDRED THIRTEENTH CONGRESS

SECOND SESSION

JULY 15, 2014

Serial No. 113–184

Printed for the use of the Committee on Foreign Affairs

Available via the World Wide Web: http://www.foreignaffairs.house.gov/ or
http://www.gpo.gov/fdsys/

U.S. GOVERNMENT PRINTING OFFICE

88–731PDF   WASHINGTON : 2014

For sale by the Superintendent of Documents, U.S. Government Printing Office
Internet: bookstore.gpo.gov   Phone: toll free (866) 512–1800; DC area (202) 512–1800
Fax: (202) 512–2104   Mail: Stop IDCC, Washington, DC 20402–0001

COMMITTEE ON FOREIGN AFFAIRS

EDWARD R. ROYCE, California, *Chairman*

SUBCOMMITTEE ON EUROPE, EURASIA, AND EMERGING THREATS

DANA ROHRABACHER, California, *Chairman*

CONTENTS

THE FUTURE OF TURKISH DEMOCRACY

TUESDAY, JULY 15, 2014

House of Representatives,
Subcommittee on Europe, Eurasia, and Emerging Threats,
Committee on Foreign Affairs,
Washington, DC.

The committee met, pursuant to notice, at 2 o'clock p.m., in room 2200 Rayburn House Office Building, Hon. Dana Rohrabacher (chairman of the subcommittee) presiding.

Mr. ROHRABACHER. The hearing will come to order, and the title of this hearing today is The Future of Turkish Democracy. Without objection, all members will have 5 legislative days to submit additional questions or extraneous material for the record. So ordered.

Just over 1 year ago, I gaveled this subcommittee for a hearing that focused on the protests that were then going on in Turkey. At the close of the hearing I stated my hope that Turkey would use the episode of turmoil that they were going through as a vehicle to move closer rather than further away from democratic government.

Today's hearing seeks to address if my hope for a democratic progress back then was well placed. Turkey is a strategically located American partner and a valued NATO ally. That is not hallow rhetoric, the fact is being demonstrated right now that Turkey is so important to us. And with the creation of the Southern Gas Corridor, Turkey is poised to become a key energy transit country for the European Union.

Turkey has also taken in a huge number of civilian refugees from Syria, most likely over 1 million men, women and children. Those of us who remember history find it heartening to see Turkey, which had been in a killing match with different parts of the Kurdish community, is now a very positive force in the Iraqi Kurdish Government and reaching out to its own Kurdish population to find areas of cooperation. Yet, the relationship between the Turkish people and the American people is built not on geostrategic calculations but on shared democratic values.

I want to make it very clear that our discussion here today, our comments and even our criticisms of the Turkish Government both former and current are not aimed at the citizens of Turkey, or are being done with great respect to the Turkish people themselves and yes, the Turkish Government. The people of the United States and the people of Turkey are friends and nothing we say today, even though there will be some criticism registered, will alter that fact.

During the Prime Minister Erdogan's more than 10 years in office he has led Turkey to tremendous economic growth, averaging more than 5 percent a year. Unfortunately political freedom in Turkey cannot be measured by the country's level of economic prosperity. The prime minister has been at times intolerant of legitimate political opposition.

The AK Party has increasingly gone down a dangerous path. And when faced with tough opposition, instead of negotiation and compromise the ruling party has often been intransigent and vengeful. Certain social media Web sites have been blocked, journalists jailed or fired, and the justice system politicized.

Let me note that in May of this year, Freedom House downgraded Turkey's freedom, or oppressed freedom ranking to not free. Those of us who count ourselves as friends of Turkey—and let me restate that I consider myself a friend of Turkey—cannot help but be alarmed by such reports. No matter what political party or leader comes to power in Turkey, liberal democracy is not possible if key civil society institutions such as freedom of the press do not function.

The United States wants Turkey to be a stable ally on the edge of the Middle East. And as the Middle East goes into such turmoil it is even more important that we have a stable Turkey, but we don't want stability at the price of democracy. Our shared national interests stem from our shared democratic values. That is and must continue to be the bedrock of the relationship between Turkey and the United States.

I would like to hear from our expert witnesses today, their views on the state of democracy on Turkey and how the leadership of this prime minister has affected the freedom of expression, the media, the minority religious groups and the economy. And lastly, how can this Congress help to ensure that Turkey is on the pathway of expanding democratic rights for all its citizens and yet remains a valued strategic partner of the United States?

I would like to thank all of our members here, and recognizing that we are blessed by having the chairman of the full committee showing a specific interest in this hearing and he is with us today. And I would ask if Chairman Royce of the full Committee on Foreign Affairs has an opening statement that he would like to make.

Mr. ROYCE. Thank you, Mr. Chairman. I would like to associate myself with your remarks, Mr. Rohrabacher, and I would like to also thank you for holding this important hearing.

An overwhelmingly Muslim country, Turkey is a NATO ally, as Mr. Rohrabacher indicated, and it has long been a secular democracy. But I too am concerned as is Mr. Rohrabacher about recent events that indicate a shift by Prime Minister Erdogan away from democratic ideals. And my concern, my concern would be as that shift occurs and it reverts to more authoritarian rule, my concern is with some of the comments that I have seen made. One reportedly stated that ''Democracy is like a bus ride. Once I get to my stop, I am getting off.''

With that kind of commentary and also with the use of strong arm tactics against opponents, this is what gives rise to concern. This approach was clearly demonstrated in the response to the 2013 protests in which—and I understand the viewpoint there, but frankly it was treated as though the head of state regarded that as illegitimate challenge. And it resorted to violence, it resorted to the dispersing of the crowds by violence and a key target was the media. You had 153 journalists injured at that time and 39 detained by the police.

Reporters Without Borders noted in their 2014 report on ''Press Freedom in the World'' that 60 journalists, around 60 journalists were in detention in Turkey in 2013, including at least 28 held in connection with their work, making the country one of the world's biggest prisons for media personnel.

In reaction to comments last year on Twitter regarding a corruption investigation involving his AKP party, Erdogan had an immediate response and it was to vilify Twitter stating, ''There is now a menace which is called Twitter. To me, social media is the worst menace to society.'' A few days later he moved to block all access to the site and followed shortly thereafter to banning access to YouTube.

Freedom of religion is also threatened. According to the 2014 United States Commission on International Religious Freedom report, ''Politically, religious freedom abuses are linked with the absence of democracy and the presence of abuses of other human rights, such as freedom of expression, association and assembly.''

Religious minorities in Turkey suffer under strict controls governing their affairs, including their ability to choose their own church leaders, to manage and raise funds, own property, and even access to their historic sites of worship. The continued closure of the Orthodox Church's Halki Seminary by the Turkish Government presents a fundamental threat to the Ecumenical Patriarchate.

Despite optimistic claims by Turkish leaders in 2011 that the revised Foundations Law would allow all church properties to be returned within a year, a majority of properties remain confiscated. In many cases the situation has actually gotten worse. Instead of returning them to their rightful owners, the Turkish Directorate General of Foundations approved the conversion of Byzantine Orthodox churches previously expropriated by the Turkish Government into mosques, and there is even legislation before the Turkish Parliament to likewise convert the Hagia Sophia church in Istanbul.

Many believe these actions constitute to eradicate the presence of the Christian heritage in Turkey since it first arrived there 2,000 years ago. That is why I am pleased that a few weeks ago the committee passed my legislation, H.R. 4347, which will not only call on Turkey to return these properties but also enact a report requirement to hold Turkish leaders accountable for progress on this issue.

By committing ourselves to acting on such legislative measures and by holding hearings on the situation in Turkey, it is my hope that Congress will send a clear message that the Turkish Government must renew its commitment to democracy and the basic human rights for all of its people. And this would be the foundation for a closer U.S.-Turkey relationship.

Thank you again, Mr. Chairman.

Mr. ROHRABACHER. Mr. Chairman, we appreciate your particular interest in this hearing and joining us today, and we appreciate your opening statement. Now have an opening statement from the ranking member, Mr. Keating.

Mr. KEATING. Thank you, Mr. Chairman, and thank you for holding this important hearing. I would like to thank today's witnesses for joining us and minority witness, Mr. Cagaptay, for your participation in what has turned out to be a very diverse panel. Thank you all.

I would also like to take a moment to recognize the Turkish hostages that are still missing over a month after they were taken from the Turkish consulate and other locations in Mosul. We hope for their safe passage back home to their families.

Turkey is an important U.S. ally in a very different part of the world, and as Ranking Member Engel and I discussed in a recent letter to the Economist, their membership in NATO cannot be understated. Mr. Chairman, if you will allow me I would like to insert that letter into the record.

Mr. ROHRABACHER. So ordered.

Mr. KEATING. Thank you, Mr. Chairman.

Nevertheless, challenges in the relationship remain. I am interested to hear our witnesses today discuss their thoughts on what happened to this so-called model partnership, the role that domestic politics plays in Turkey's foreign policy decisions and how this ultimately affects the U.S.

Like all democracies, including our own, there are bumps in the road. But with upcoming Presidential elections in Turkey, it is important to gauge how long these bumps in Turkey will persist and what impact they will ultimately have. It seems as though in the preceding months and years we witnessed the steady intensification of crackdowns on protests. Authorities have at times even arrested doctors treating injured protesters, and lawyers demanding more accountability and transparency within the judiciary.

We have also witnessed the blocking of important communication tools such as Twitter and YouTube. Most recently, many observers have raised valid concerns that the electoral dominance of Prime Minister Erdogan's AK Party will result, as some observers argue, in a Turkey that is now essentially a one-party system. They say that opposition parties can no longer voice, much less influence, decision making.

These issues take on special importance to Congress. Not because we have any interest in meddling in Turkey's internal affairs, but simply because we represent hundreds of U.S. citizens of Turkish origin, American companies, as well as other groups who continue to be affected by these decisions and the overall instability that these policies create.

The United States and Turkey are also dealing with serious issues of mutual concern over terrorism and extremism which is bubbling up right at Turkey's border. As we weigh our own international budget priorities in Congress, we need to understand the role that Turkey's internal dynamics have on our own counterterrorism initiatives in the region. It is unclear to what extent Turkey's internal disputes have disrupted our cooperation in the areas of counterterrorism and mutual defense, but I doubt that there has been no impact at all.

To cite just a few perplexing matters, in just the last few years the top brass of the Turkish military, the first line of defense against the extremists in the region, were imprisoned then released. Weapons interdictions along the Syrian-Turkish border continue to occur, and allegedly, recordings pointing to large-scale bribes between the prime minister, his family, party officials and Iranian businessmen may have larger implications for our policy on Iran and sanctions.

Our job in this subcommittee is to look into these incidents, their veracity, the implications that they might have for the U.S., and I am happy we are doing so today. That being said, the actual resolution of these disputes and any attempt to mend longstanding fault lines based on religion, ethnicity or ideology can only be completed by the Turks and the Turks alone.

I believe the Turks through civil society engagement and diverse economic activities can overcome many of the obstacles that the headlines are focusing on today. Great strides have been made to open up the Turkish economy, trade and culture to others. This is a positive sign as economic security and human rights issues are all interlinked, and I believe that one can propel the other in this case.

I know that the administration, Members of Congress, the vibrant Turkish diaspora here in the U.S., and the Government and the people of Turkey all deeply value U.S.-Turkey relationships. Despite concerns about human rights, I am encouraged by the many energetic discussions taking place in Turkey and their implications for the future of Turkey's democracy and I look forward to hearing our witnesses and their perspectives on Turkey's future.

With that Mr. Chairman, I yield my time back.

Mr. ROHRABACHER. Did you have time to yield back?

Mr. KEATING. I did, 2 seconds. Two seconds.

Mr. ROHRABACHER. And it is the intent of the Chair to break after we have one more opening statement and then to return here at 15 minutes to 3 o'clock to hear the testimony and to proceed with the hearing.

Mr. Sires?

Mr. SIRES. For the sake of time I will just summarize a little bit of my concerns. I have concerns of the way the government has been behaving. I share the comments that my colleague made. I am concerned about the hard lines he seems to be taking all the time to the Cyprus issue. I am concerned about the amount of troops that Turkey has in Cyprus.

And, quite frankly, I understand that they are a good friend, members of NATO, but at the end of the day I think that their behavior at least ought to be the sign in some areas. So I thank you for giving me the opportunity to speak.

Mr. ROHRABACHER. Thank you very much. And this hearing is now in, not adjourned, it is in recess. There we go.

[Recess.]

Mr. ROHRABACHER. I do not believe that the ranking member will be upset if I proceed with just the introduction of the witnesses so when he gets here we will be ready to have the testimony. So I call this hearing back into order, and I want to apologize about if I mispronounce names. With a name like Rohrabacher I have had my name mispronounced forever. But it is okay.

Okay, our first witness today is Nate Schenkkan—okay, got it—who is a program officer for Freedom House. He has been closely following media freedom in Turkey and coauthored the Freedom House's special report on Turkey earlier this year. He has previously worked as a journalist in Central Asia and earned his masters degree from Columbia University.

We then have with us Professor Elizabeth Prodromou—okay, thank you. She is a visiting associate professor at the Fletcher School of Law and Diplomacy at Tufts University. She also previously served as vice chairman of the United States Commission on International Religious Freedom and earned a doctorate in political science from MIT.

I would also like to welcome back Dr. Soner Cagaptay—got it—who is the director of Turkish Research Program at the Washington Institute for Near East Policy. He is a widely published expert on U.S.-Turkish relations and who has regularly testified before Congress. He has earned his doctorate from Yale.

Then we have Mr. Hakan Tasci—got it—and he is executive director of Tuskon, the U.S. representative office of a large confederation of Turkish businesses which represent thousands of companies in Turkey. And before his current job he taught economics at the University of North Carolina at Chapel Hill and earned his masters degree from Bilkent University in Turkey.

And then we have Dr. Kilic Kanat. He is a resident scholar at SETA Foundation here in Washington. He also is assistant professor of political science at Pennsylvania State University at Erie, and the professor had earned a Ph.D. in political science from Syracuse University.

And I would welcome all of you today and also express my gratitude to you for your testimony. And we will wait another couple minutes, but in the meantime let me just explain that if you could keep your remarks to 5 minutes you can submit remarks that long for the record. But if you could put them down to 5 minutes we could then get to some questions and answers and perhaps some dialogue.

And I am a little bit hesitant about starting the actual testimony until one of our minority members are here. So with that said, well, I could tell a few jokes if you would like. So you know about the story about the woman who set up, an elderly woman who set up a pretzel stand outside of a large business. Well, it could be in Turkey for all that matter. And it was a big modern business building, and every day a businessman would stop by and—oh, you are never going to get to hear the end of this joke.

With your permission I will finish the joke.

Mr. KEATING. I have heard it before.

Mr. ROHRABACHER. He has. So every day he stops by and he puts 50 cents into her plate and then he runs into the building. But he never takes a pretzel. This goes on for over a year. And finally, as he puts 50 cents into the plate she grabs him by the arm, and he looks into her face and he says, you probably want to know why for a full year I have been putting 50 cents into your plate but I have never taken a pretzel. And she says, well, no, I just want to tell you pretzels are up to 75 cents.

All right. They get it. Gratitude. I have already introduced the witnesses, and with your permission we will proceed with the testimony.

STATEMENT OF MR. NATE SCHENKKAN, PROGRAM OFFICER, EURASIA PROGRAMS, FREEDOM HOUSE

Mr. SCHENKKAN. Thank you, Mr. Chairman. Thank you to the subcommittee for the invitation to speak today. My opening remarks touch on the most recent developments in 2014 affecting fundamental freedoms in Turkey. This is a summary of my full testimony.

I think the statements of Chairman Rohrabacher and Chairman Royce on the Gezi protests captured well the sense that the government missed an opportunity to acknowledge the large minority in Turkey that was frustrated with its lack of voice in an increasingly majoritarian system. Since the time when the government halted the Gezi protests with police force in July 2013, the government has grown even more intolerant and dismissive of criticism. This tendency intensified following the corruption investigation announced on December 17th, 2013, which implicated leading members of the government. The December 17th investigation sparked a furious effort on the part of the government to suppress the investigation and the ensuing leaks.

In this effort, the government has directly targeted the ability of journalists and others to access and disseminate information, and I would like to describe some of those key negative steps in 2014. First, amendments to the already repressive law governing Internet services, Law 5651, which make it easier and faster to block Web sites and to determine the identities of Internet users.

Two, the complete blocking of Twitter and YouTube 1 week prior to the March 30th local elections. Although the Constitutional Court overturned both of these blocks after the election, they still violated freedom of expression and the right to access information especially during a political campaign.

Three, and the most disturbing development is the new law granting special powers to the National Intelligence Organization, or MIT. The law entitles the MIT to collect all information, documents or data, from any entity in Turkey. It makes publishing information about the MIT punishable by 3 to 9 years in prison. It places the MIT and its employees outside of normal structures of legal accountability. This supra-legal National Intelligence Organization is a grave threat to Turkish democracy.

There also continue to be serious problems with freedom of association and assembly that I will mention quickly. The prosecution especially of members of Taksim Solidarity, the original organizers of the first Gezi Park protest, on the absurd charge of founding a criminal organization.

Now a few words directly on the subject of the panel of The Future of Turkish Democracy. Like most people I expect Prime Minister Erdogan will win the Presidential election in August, likely in the first round. Then his first priority will be to create de facto Presidential rule, and then following the June 2015 parliamentary elections, a de jure Presidential system through constitutional reform.

A Presidential system is not inherently bad, and Turkey needs a new Constitution. But given Mr. Erdogan's ''with us or against us'' style of governance, I fear constitutional reform will be neither inclusive nor consultative. Mr. Erdogan sees himself as leading a revolution against elites and outside powers, and a revolution requires constantly creating enemies, real or imagined, who must be defeated.

I fear Mr. Erdogan's presidency will sharpen divisions within Turkish society and further weaken institutions in favor of personalized rule. This will harm human rights and fundamental freedoms, and also the rule of law and economic management.

If there is a slim silver lining from the last 13 months, it is that the U.S. Government no longer casts Turkey as a model democracy. For many years of AK Party rule, U.S. policy toward Turkey ignored and overlooked highly visible problems with human rights, democracy and rule of law. This exercise in positive thinking did not serve Turkey and it did not serve the United States.

The new frankness about Turkey's internal dynamics offers an opportunity for the U.S. to make supporting Turkey's democracy a serious part of its policy planning. The European Union remains the best mechanism for the U.S. to support the development in Turkey of effective institutions with checks and balances. Right now Turkey's accession has lost momentum. The U.S. has been committed to Turkey's EU membership, but primarily through rhetorical support through to what is treated as an EU-Turkey process.

The U.S. should elevate Turkey's accession as an urgent strategic priority and create a high level policy dialogue with the Turkish Government in consultation with the EU to deploy U.S. support where it is needed. A good immediate step toward accession would be lifting EU member state blocks on opening chapters 23 and 24 of the EU acquis on Judiciary and Fundamental Rights and Justice, Freedom and Security. The best way for the U.S. to support democracy in Turkey is by integrating democracy and human rights into the strategic bilateral policy relationship just as security and trade have been integrated. Thank you, Mr. Chairman.

[The prepared statement of Mr. Schenkkan follows:]

Hearing on "The Future of Turkish Democracy"

Testimony by Nate Schenkkan, Program Officer

Freedom House

**Before The Subcommittee on Europe, Eurasia and Emerging Threats,
Foreign Affairs Committee of the United States House of Representatives,
July 15, 2014**

Mr. Chairman and distinguished members of the subcommittee:

Thank you for this important hearing. Given the monumental events of the last year in Turkey, and the upcoming presidential elections that will shape the direction of Turkey's politics for decades to come, the subcommittee has made a timely decision in taking up the question of Turkey's democracy and where it is headed.

It has been just over thirteen months since the Gezi Park protests began. Especially in the early days of the protests, there were many who saw them as an opportunity for Turkey: a chance for the government to strengthen democracy by compromising with a large minority frustrated with its lack of voice in an increasingly majoritarian system.

Unfortunately in the past year the government has not taken that opportunity. Since halting the Gezi protests with overwhelming police force in July 2013, the government has grown even more intolerant and dismissive of criticism. This tendency intensified following the launch of the major corruption investigation on December 17, 2013, which implicated leading members of the government and was followed by leaked recordings of government officials apparently engaged in massive corruption.

I want to highlight here several of the key examples of how the government has sought to suppress dissent, with a special focus on the media.

First, it is important to understand that the chief mechanism of control of most media in Turkey is not a law but the relationships between media owners and government officials, especially the Prime Minister. The country's largest media outlets are owned by corporate holding companies that depend heavily on government procurement contracts in areas like construction, housing, transport, and logistics. This makes them very vulnerable to government pressure, and incentivizes holding companies to use their media arms as lobbying firms for major government contracts.

To give one example, certain of the conversations released after December 17 involve the owners of major construction firms that were seeking to win contracts to build Istanbul's multibillion-dollar third airport. The leaked conversations show that the owners were directed by a government minister to contribute hundreds of millions of dollars of their money to a "pool" to buy one of the country's largest and most important media companies, Sabah-ATV. The owners would then be expected to provide positive coverage of the government. This has created the expression in Turkish "*havuz medyası*" – literally "the pool media" – to describe corporate owners whose media properties are in service of the government.

This relationship between corporate owners and the government creates a clear conflict of interest that the government exploits. In other recordings released after December 17, Prime Minister Erdoğan is heard berating a top manager of the television station HaberTürk for running coverage of opposition politicians on his news channel. The prime minister has publicly confirmed one of these incidents, when he demanded that the manager remove a ticker from the bottom of the screen describing an opposition politician's speech.

For years before Gezi, journalists in Turkey had been describing the prime minister's phone calls to have coverage changed and individual journalists fired for speaking out in ways that displeased him. When more than 80 journalists were fired during the Gezi protests for critical coverage, therefore, it was a continuation of a process that had begun years before.

The government's direct leverage over media ownership is coupled with a very repressive set of legal tools that are actively used to punish dissent. These include criminal and civil defamation laws, which the government continues to use very widely against all sorts of protected speech. Prime Minister Erdoğan himself has filed hundreds of defamation suits. In one of many examples, on January 20, 2014, the prime minister won compensation in a libel suit against author İhsan Eliaçık who had accused Erdoğan of being a "dictator, a corrupt leader, provocateur, liar and arrogant" on his Twitter account during the Gezi Park protests.

The European Court of Human Rights has ruled, in Tuşalp v. Turkey, 2012, that using civil defamation laws to afford greater protection to public officials is a violation of Article 10 of the European Convention on Human Rights, which is legally binding upon Turkey as a signatory.

The government can even dictate to media organizations which stories not to cover. Most recently on June 17 this year the Radio and Television Higher Council (RTÜK) issued a ban on reporting on the capture of Turkey's diplomatic representatives in Mosul, Iraq by the Islamic State of Iraq and Syria, or ISIS. This blackout remained in effect as of July 11.

The country's harsh anti-terrorism laws create another major limit on freedom of speech. Despite a series of judicial reforms, these laws remain broad and susceptible to abuse. Under these laws, reporting on or interviewing members of terrorist or illegal organizations can result in years of pre-trial detention followed by long jail sentences. Although Turkey is no longer the world's leading jailer of journalists thanks to a reform in spring 2014 that released dozens of journalists who had served years in pre-trial detention, it is important to note that in most cases these are only conditional releases, and the original charges remain open against these journalists.

The December 17 investigation, which has been clearly supported by the Gülen movement that once allied itself with Mr. Erdoğan's government, has created a furious purge of alleged Gülenists inside and outside of the government that is still ongoing, as well as a wave of repressive legislation. Several key parts of this effort directly target the ability of journalists and others to access and disseminate information.

One of the key steps was the passage of amendments to the law governing blocking internet services, Law 5651. The new amendments mandated the retention of user data for 1-2 years, to be specified by later legislation; required Internet Service Providers to join an "ISP Union" that would not be able to write its own bylaws and will be essentially under government control; and made it possible for the government to block individual URLs. The original legislation also allowed websites to be blocked without a court order, although after President Gül's intervention there will be a special court created to handle blocking requests. It is unclear what rights users and website owners will have to contest blocking requests. The clear objective of the new law is to make it easier and faster to block websites and to determine the identities of internet users.

Again it is important to note that the European Court of Human Rights had ruled in 2012 in Yildirim v. Turkey that the earlier version of Law 5651 violated the European Convention on Human Rights by lacking sufficient safeguards against abuses. The new version of 5651 has not resolved this problem, and indeed it has made it worse.

In another violation of the Yildirim ruling, in the week prior to the March 30 local elections, the government completely blocked both Twitter and YouTube in Turkey prior to the March 30 local elections. Twitter and YouTube had been the two main platforms for disseminating leaked recordings of corruption. Although the Constitutional Court overturned both blockings after the election, they still violated freedom of expression and the right to access information, especially during a political campaign.

The most disturbing legislative development following the December 17 investigation is the new law granting special powers to the National Intelligence Organization, or MİT. The law entitles the MİT to collect all information, documents or data from any entity in Turkey. The law does not refer to a warrant or other judicial process for approving this collection. Interference with the activities of the MİT, for instance by refusing a request for data, is punishable by 2-5 years in prison. Obtaining information about the MİT is punishable by 4-10 years in prison. Publishing information about the MİT by any form of media including social media is punishable by 3-9 years in prison. These provisions are a clear threat to journalists' and citizens' rights to freedom of expression, access to information, and privacy.

The law also places the MİT and its employees outside of normal structures of accountability. Article 8 of the law says that any requests coming from the MİT will be considered superior to all other legal obligations, and that any person complying with these requests will be relieved of legal liability for violations of the law created by compliance. The article explicitly states that this law is superior to any other laws on this subject.

This supra-legal National Intelligence Organization constitutes a grave threat to Turkish democracy.

Most of my testimony has focused on freedom of the media and of expression, but I also want to mention an important case concerning freedom of association and assembly.

The prosecution of the members of Taksim Solidarity – the group that organized the original small Gezi Park protests in May 2013 – is especially disturbing and should be a matter of serious Congressional interest. In a case that opened last month, 26 Taksim Solidarity members are facing charges related to the protests. Most disturbingly, five of the members are being charged with "forming an illegal organization," a crime that can carry up to 15 and a half years in prison. Civil society is concerned that this case could eventually be used to prosecute others through guilt-by-association.

Finally, I will turn to the topic of the panel, the future of Turkish democracy. Like most people I believe Prime Minister Erdoğan will win the presidential election in August, quite likely in the first round. It is clear that his top priority is to create first *de facto* presidential rule, and then following the June 2015 parliamentary elections, a *de jure* presidential system through constitutional reform.

A presidential system is not inherently bad, and Turkey needs a new constitution. But given Mr. Erdoğan's "with us or against us" style of governance, I fear constitutional reform will be neither inclusive nor consultative. Mr. Erdoğan sees himself as leading a revolution against secularist elites and outside powers. And a revolution requires constantly creating enemies--real or imagined--who must be defeated. I fear Mr. Erdoğan's presidency will sharpen divisions within Turkish society and further weaken institutions in favor of personalized rule. This will harm human rights and fundamental freedoms, and also the rule of law and economic management.

If there is a slim silver lining from the last 13 months, it is that the U.S. government no longer casts Turkey as a model democracy. For many years of AK Party rule, U.S. policy towards Turkey ignored highly visible problems with human rights, democracy, and rule of law. This exercise in positive thinking did not serve Turkey and it did not serve the United States. The new

13

frankness about Turkey's internal dynamics offers an opportunity for the U.S. to make Turkey's democracy a serious part of its policy planning.

The European Union remains the best mechanism for the U.S. to support the development in Turkey of effective independent institutions with checks and balances. Yet right now Turkey's accession has lost momentum. The U.S. has been committed to Turkey's E.U. membership, but primarily through rhetorical support to what is treated as an E.U.-Turkey process. The U.S. should elevate Turkey's accession as a strategic priority and designate a high-level official specifically tasked with accession to guide U.S. strategy in support of Turkey's membership. The U.S. should request an appropriate-level interlocutor from the Turkish side with an agreed schedule for high-level dialogue on progress. Designated working-level groups from both sides should meet more frequently. This process should be transparent to and inclusive of Turkish civil society. It is important that it be in consultation with the E.U. through an interlocutor who can brief on the E.U. perspective and support the efforts of the working group to advance the process.

Turkey's E.U. membership should not be treated as a "nice if it happens" outcome – it should be regarded as a top-level priority for the United States in the region, on par with security and economic goals. A good immediate step towards this goal would be helping lift E.U. member state blocks on accession and opening chapters 23 and 24 of the E.U. acquis on Judiciary and Fundamental Rights and Justice, Freedom and Security. Turkey's process for E.U. accession has been long and it will still stretch longer, but every step along the way makes an important contribution to securing democracy in Turkey.

The best way for the U.S. to support democracy in Turkey is by integrating democracy and human rights into the bilateral policy relationship, just as security and trade have been integrated. The United States' long-term vision of its relationship with Turkey should be built on the country's institutional and democratic development.

Mr. ROHRABACHER. Thank you very much for your testimony, and we will have questions and answers after everyone is complete.

STATEMENT OF ELIZABETH H. PRODROMOU, PH.D., VISITING ASSOCIATE PROFESSOR OF CONFLICT RESOLUTION, THE FLETCHER SCHOOL OF LAW AND DIPLOMACY, TUFTS UNIVERSITY

Ms. PRODROMOU. Good afternoon and thank you as well. I want to express my thanks to the subcommittee and to the full committee for this hearing. Having served as a commissioner and vice chair on the U.S. Commission on International Religious Freedom, I am also, currently, as a member of the Secretary of State's working group on Religion and U.S. Foreign Policy, I am very heartened by the committee's attention to the matters that bring us here this afternoon.

I am going to begin by offering some general remarks and then some very specific data points that focus particularly on the issue of religious freedom and the rights of religious minorities in Turkey, particularly as these relate to broader questions of media freedom and democracy as a whole.

The starting point, I think, the best starting point is to reference the international human rights standards such as the Universal Declaration of Human Rights and the International Covenant on Civil and Political Rights. Both of these unequivocally identify the right to religious freedom, freedom of thought, conscience and religion as a universal human right and that includes freedom to change one's religion or belief, freedom either alone or within community in public or in private, to manifest a belief as well as teaching, practice, worship and observance.

So measured within this context, it is fair to say, I think, that there have been some evidences of minor progress in Turkey during the period since the AKP was elected in 2002. When it comes to the rights of religious minorities in the country, I would say that that the progress largely lies within the context of a discursive expansion in the form of a far more public discussion of previous taboo issues concerning violations against the rights of religious minorities.

And then the second is what I would call minor improvements, cosmetic and episodic in nature that have been designed to loosen restrictions on religious freedom for Turkey's religious minority communities largely regarding the rights of the country's tiny Christian community and very small Jewish community. And within this second category we could include the 2011 property rights law on foundations.

But even here the progress has been very, very small. Only 23 percent of applications for return of properties have been accepted and that means that 77 percent of applications for the return of properties to individuals and groups belonging to religious minorities have been arbitrarily rejected by the government. So measured against these small improvements, I think the real sobering picture is as follows, and that is that there has been a real failure to make any kind of substantive legal and institutional changes that would ensure that all of Turkey's citizens regardless of what religious faith community they belong to are seen as equal before the law.

And there are a few emblematic examples, I think, that underscore this point and which speak to again the corrosive effects of religious freedom violations on Turkey's democracy. Some of these were mentioned in brief in the opening remarks, but I think they are worth emphasizing. A quite aggressive Islamization strategy that has been based on the conversion of Christian churches into mosques over the last 2½ years alone, the conversion of the church of St. Sophia in Trabzon, and then as St. Sophia, at Isnik, into functioning mosques, and then the declared commitment of the AKP government with no response to the contrary by opposition party members to convert the church of Aghia Sophia in Istanbul into a functioning mosque. And that is actually a UNESCO World Heritage site.

Second example. The continuing interference in the internal governance structures of Christian and Jewish minority communities in Turkey by the Turkish state imposing arbitrary citizenship requirements for election to hierarchical positions. And third example, prohibitions continue on religious education and especially on the training of clergy that Greek Orthodox Theological School of Halki remains closed after more than 40 years, and the prime minister as well as senior members of his government declared publicly that there is absolutely no legal impediment to reopening the Halki school. That it is a political issue, pure and simple.

Two other examples, and I will move to close. One particularly concerning example, the Turkish state's continuing use of a racial coding system for its religious minority communities. They are called the ancestry codes, and accordingly Greeks, Armenians, Syriacs and others presumably in that category, Roman Catholics and Protestants, are coded 1 through 5 by the Ministry of Education, the Ministry of Information and the Population Directorate, and that racial coding system has been designed to exclude those groups from government as well as to facilitate massive property expropriations on citizen revocations.

And then finally, the comprehensive religious cleansing policy that has been pursued systematically for 40 years by the Turkish Armed Forces and the Turkish Cypriot authorities in Turkish-occupied Cyprus. It will be 40 years on this coming 20th of July that the Turkish Armed Forces set up occupation on the north of the island. And when I say religious cleansing, I mean the cleansing of any kind of presence of Christian communities in the occupied north. That is living human beings as well as religious patrimony, everything from churches, monasteries, cemeteries. They have been desecrated. There has been a systematic looting and black market sale of moveable artifacts from those properties, and there are continuing limitations on the ability of those tiny, less than 400 members of the Christian community there to worship.

What does all this mean? All this is very sobering, I think, for the direction of Turkish democracy. And as my copanelist mentioned, I think there is every reason to be concerned about the immediate future. The move to a Presidential system is likely to bode very poorly for religious freedom rights for minorities in Turkey, and also concerningly, the secular opposition in Turkey has indeed been supportive. In fact, they are the architects of most of the legislature that exists in Turkey that have violated the rights of the country's religious minorities.

In terms of the United States and our commitment to religious freedom, I would reinforce the remarks of my copanelist and also encourage the committee to move expeditiously for the passage of House Resolution 4347, and also to work with the U.S. Commission on International Religious Freedom around issues related to the violations of religious minorities in Turkey. Thank you.

[The prepared statement of Ms. Prodromou follows:]

Remarks by Dr. Elizabeth H. Prodromou
Visiting Associate Professor of Conflict Resolution
The Fletcher School of Law and Diplomacy, Tufts University

**Testimony to the U.S. House of Representatives Committee on Foreign Affairs
Subcommittee on Europe, Eurasia, and Emerging Threats**

Congressman Dana Rohrabacher (R-CA), Chairman

Hearing on "The Future of Turkish Democracy"

**July 15, 2014 at 2 p.m.
Room 2200, Rayburn House Office Building**

Mr. Chairman and Members of the Subcommittee,

Good afternoon. Mr. Chairman and Members of the Subcommittee. Allow me to thank you for the invitation to brief you today on the future of democracy in Turkey. I respectfully request that my written comments, from which I will draw for this testimony, be submitted into the Congressional Record.

As a former Commissioner and Vice Chair of the US Commission on International Religious Freedom and as a current member of the Secretary of State's Religion and Foreign Policy Working Group, I am heartened by the Subcommittee's recognition that media freedom, the rights of religious minorities, and the vitality of civil society, are crucial issues for the health and quality of democracy in Turkey, as well as for Turkey's capacity to play a consistent, positive, and effective role in partnership with the United States and NATO in confronting serious threats to stability in Europe and Eurasia.

In an effort to respect the time limitations on this hearing and well aware of the expertise of my fellow panelists, let me offer some general remarks and, then, specific data points, that focus on the rights of religious minorities in Turkey. The most constructive way of thinking about the rights of religious minorities in Turkey, as part of an overall assessment of democracy in Turkey, is within the context of international human rights standards established in foundational documents such as the Universal Declaration of Human Rights and the International Covenant on Civil and Political Rights, amongst others. International human rights standards unequivocally identified the right to freedom of thought, conscience, and religion, including the freedom to change one's religion or belief, as well as freedom, either alone or within a community, in public and private, to manifest religious belief in teaching, practice, worship and observance. (Paraphrase from the UDHR and ICCPR).

Measured against these international human rights standards, it is fair to say that there is evidence of some progress in Turkey during the period since the AKP (Justice and Development Party) was elected into government. The progress has come largely in two areas: the first is what I would call discursive improvements, in the form of a breaking of the long-held taboos in the Turkish government, media, and civil society, on discussions regarding systematic and egregious violations in the rights of religious minorities in Turkey (e.g. discussion of the Armenian Genocide, cleansing of Greek Orthodox Christians and the suffocation of the Ecumenical Patriarchate, through mechanisms of violence and non-violence);

and the second is what I would call remedial efforts designed to loosen restrictions on religious freedom for Turkey's religious minority communities, particularly the rights of the country's tiny Christian minority communities (they comprise less than 1 percent of Turkey's overall population). The progress in these two areas has been widely reported, particularly when it comes to the 2011 liberalization in the law regulating property rights (return and compensation) for the country's religious minorities (return and compensation of vast amounts of property expropriated and/or transferred by the Turkish state from the Greek, Armenian, and Syriac Christian communities), and when it comes to permission by the Turkish state authorities for celebrations at well-known Christian religious sites, such as the Greek Orthodox Sumela Monastery and the Armenian Apostolic Monastery of Akhtamar. The invitation to leaders of the country's religious minority communities (e.g. Ecumenical Patriarch Bartholomew, Kuryakos Ergun, head of the Syriac Mor Gabriel Monastery) to address the Turkish Parliament as part of the constitutional reform process, also suggested the possibility for improving the rights of religious minorities in Turkey.

However, despite signals, suggestions, and hopes for improvements in religious freedom conditions for Turkey's religious minority communities, the facts on the ground reveal a sobering picture of no substantive change—by that, I mean the failure to make legal and institutional changes necessary to ensure that all of Turkey's citizens are treated equally before the law—and, indeed, worrisome changes of deterioration in the rights of religious minorities. Indeed, put simply, if one uses religious freedom for Turkey's minority communities as a metric for the overall robustness and quality of democracy in Turkey, there is cause for grave concern. Three issues illustrate my point:

1. An Islamization strategy built on the conversation of Christian Churches into mosques (e.g. St. Sophia in Trabzon and Iznik/Nicaea, and the declared commitment of the AKP government to convert the Byzantine Cathedral of Aghia Sophia—a UNESCO World Heritage site) into a mosque, and on the destruction of any physical footprint of the religious patrimony of Christianity in Turkish-occupied Cyprus.
2. The continuing interference in the internal governance structures of Christian and Jewish minorities in Turkey (e.g. imposition of arbitrary citizenship requirements for election to the Ecumenical Patriarchate and the Armenian and Syriac Patriarchates).
3. Prohibitions on religious education and, especially, training of clergy, which ensures the disappearance of hierarchs and priests and, therefore, the annihilation of Christian communities which, by their nature, depend on religious orders. Especially emblematic is the ongoing closure of the Greek Orthodox Theological School of Halki (40-plus years closed) on the Island of Heybeliada, a reality that is purely political and unrelated to legal limitations (e.g. public statements to this effect last year, by both PM Erdogan and members of his government).
4. Failure to bring to justice and/or to prosecute and/or convict perpetrators of violence against members of Turkey's Christian communities, and the troubling rise of anti-Semitism in Turkey (e.g. statements by members of the government, in Turkish state and private media outlets).
5. Turkish state's use of racial coding system for religious minorities: Ancestry Codes of Greeks, Armenians, Jews, Syriacs, Others (Roman Catholics and Protestants) as 1 through 5, by the Ministry of Education, Ministry of Information, and the Population Directorate.
6. The comprehensive religious cleansing policy perpetrated by the Turkish Armed Forces, with support from the Turkish Cypriot authorities, in Turkish-occupied Cyprus. July 20th marks the 40th year of Turkey's occupation of northern Cyprus, and the systematic cleansing of any Christian presence in Turkish-occupied Cyprus proceeds apace. Eg.s: desecration of Greek, Armenian, and Maronite Christian religious sites, the looting and black-marketeering of religious icons and art, the arbitrary limitations on rights of worship for the tiny, surviving community of

Greek Orthodox enclaved in the Rizokarpassos area in the northern part of Cyprus, as well as systematic denial of requests by the Turkish military and Turkish-Cypriot authorities, for religious services by Christians seeking to cross the Green Line.

Measured against the symbolic and episodic improvements in the rights of religious minority communities in Turkey over the past 11-or-so years, there is a broader pattern of continuing policies of economic/property disenfranchisement of Christian (and, more recently, Jewish) minorities, state interference in the internal governance and education of religious communities, institutionalized and informal racist bias and discrimination against religious minorities, and continuing religious cleansing of Christians from Turkish-occupied Cyprus. In a word, religious freedom is a sobering metric of the democracy deficits in Turkey's institutions of governance and Turkey's political leadership (both Islamist/AKP and Kemalist/CHP/MHP).

Consequently, I respectfully suggest that this Subcommittee consider ways to encourage improvements in the legal and institutional frameworks necessary to ensure that all of Turkey's citizens enjoy full equality before the law. Freedom of thought, conscience and religion or belief is inextricably tied to and refracted in media freedom and a vibrant civil society—in Turkey and elsewhere. Likewise, the strength of Turkey's democracy—particularly when it comes to rule of law and equality before the law for religious minority communities—is inextricably connected to Turkey's will and capacity to cooperate with the United States and NATO allies in confronting some of the most pernicious and serious threats (e.g. sectarian and communal violence, religious terrorism, and authoritarian forms of governance) to the Eurasian security environment.

Holding Turkey to international standards and to the expectations of a US partner and NATO ally make immanent strategic and moral sense.

I thank you for your attention.

STATEMENT OF SONER CAGAPTAY, PH.D., BEYER FAMILY FELLOW AND DIRECTOR, TURKISH RESEARCH PROGRAM, THE WASHINGTON INSTITUTE FOR NEAR EAST POLICY

Mr. CAGAPTAY. Thank you, Mr. Chairman, and thank you, members of the committee, for giving me the opportunity to testify on developments in Turkey and their implications for U.S. policy. The following is a summary of my prepared remarks.

Obviously Turkey is an important country for us. It is a NATO ally, but it is also a country that borders vital U.S. interests in Ukraine, Russia, Iraq and Syria and therefore is an important partner to the United States with regards to U.S. policy in each of these countries. With these developments in mind, Turkey's long term stability matters to the United States.

In this regard, I think we have seen significant progress in Turkey in the last decade. The country has been transformed dramatically in the economic sense, rising as a stable and wealthy nation. The Turks had experienced a decade of prosperity when all of their neighbors went through economic and political downturn and some even experienced war. And as a result of this transformation, Turkey now is in even a better position to be a prime partner for the United Stated given its robust economy.

As I point out in my monograph, ''The Rise of Turkey''—if I can make a shameless plug—Turkey has become a majority middle class society in the last decade and this has huge ramifications. This is a country now that is on the cusp of becoming history's first large Muslim majority, a universally literate society. The country is connected to a global society in ways that cannot be reversed, and these are refreshing developments.

There are also comforting improvements in terms of religious freedoms in Turkey, especially for non-Muslim communities. As my colleague, Dr. Prodromou, pointed out, the government has started restoring property belonging to church and synagogue foundations to its rightful owners, so far totaling about $1 billion of property. Obviously progress has been made and there is still progress that can be made and I think we should encourage that process.

These are key accomplishments for which Turkey's Government, AKP government and its Prime Minister Erdogan deserve credit. But I also have to add that there is a darker side to Erdogan's legacy and that is when it comes to the issue of freedoms. Ironically, while Turkey has become more prosperous under the AKP, simultaneously it has also become less free.

As measured by international indices, the country's record on liberties improved significantly when the AKP came to power in 2002 in conjunction with the country's work to qualify for EU accession, but then somehow it stagnated and then took a nose dive somewhere around the end of the last decade. According to Freedom House, Turkey was, for example, ranked 58 out of 100 in terms of press freedoms, 100 being the least free, zero being the most free. That was in 2001 before the AKP came to power. The country's record improved in 2005, it went up to 48. But then it declined, hitting 62 in 2013. So in terms of freedom of expression, Turkey is worse off than it was before the AKP.

Despite being through a democratic process, I think this is a party that governs in authoritarian fashion. It is intolerant of dissent and opposition as we have seen most prominently during the 2013 Gezi Park rallies as well as the bans on YouTube and Twitter.

A second alarming concern obviously is Turkey's pivot to the Middle East. That is a concern for the United States in the sense that this pivot has met challenges. Before the AKP, the Turks thought of themselves as a European country placed next to the Middle East. They were not from there, they just lived there.

This perception was challenged by the AKP elite who decided that the path to great power and influence for Turkey was through the Middle East rather than Europe, and that pivot turned out to be a miscalculation a decade later. With the exception of the Kurds, Turkey has no allies in the Middle East. Not only that, it borders enemies from the Assad regime to ISIS, Islamic State.

And among the many problems I think that Turkey's pivot to the Middle East has caused is ISIS to the grave threat it wants to establish a Taliban-like state along Turkey's longest land border, 800 miles of border with Iraq and Syria. Nobody wants Taliban as a neighbor. Nobody wants Taliban presence in the Middle East, which suggests that Ankara, Washington and NATO will work together against this threat and this will cement a strong U.S.-Turkey relationship, and in my view for years to come because what is in Turkey's interest is in the interest of the United States.

There are other reasons, I think, to be optimistic about Turkey's future. One is the rise of the middle class, which has grown as result of the AKP's economic policies and which is challenging its style of governance, and also the opposition, Republican People's Party, which is slowly but surely turning into a liberal movement. Recently the State Department awarded party deputy Safak Pavey with International Woman of Courage Award, recognizing the party's commitment to gender equality and democracy.

Turkey's trajectory, Mr. Chairman and members of the committee, points toward democracy, and the Turkish people need the European Union to drive further reform at home. And I think the ISIS threat has caused many Turks to clamor for the day when their country stayed out of the Middle East and looked to Europe.

So we stand at an opportune moment for a pivot. Washington should capitalize on this, relying on Turkey in combating ISIS as well as promoting the country's repositioning toward Europe. The Middle East may not have panned out the way the Turks hoped, but Turkey can still be a major power. It can be a major European power. Turkey is of vital interest to Europe and therefore to the United States. Its location, its proclivity to capitalism and democracy make it an important ally. Washington and Ankara share interests and Turkey's path will have great strategic importance to the United States in situations ranging from Ukraine to Iraq and Syria for years to come. Thank you very much.

[The prepared statement of Mr. Cagaptay follows:]

Statement of Soner Cagaptay, Ph.D.
Beyer Family Fellow/Director, Turkish Research Program
Washington Institute for Near East Policy

Testimony before the House Committee on Foreign Affairs
Subcommittee on Europe, Eurasia, and Emerging Threats:
"The Future of Turkish Democracy"

Tuesday, July 12, 2014

Thank you, Mr. Chairman and members of the Committee for giving me the opportunity to testify on developments in Turkey and their implications for U.S. policy. The following is a summary of my prepared remarks.

Turkey, a NATO member state, is an important ally for to the United States. Turkey borders vital U.S. interests in Ukraine, Iran, Iraq and Syria, and acts as a key partner for Washington in regards to each of these countries. With these developments in mind, *Turkey's long term stability matters to the U.S.*

In the past decade, Turkey has outperformed its neighbors, rising as a *stable and wealthy nation.* While all of their neighbors experienced economic meltdown, political instability, and some even war, the Turks have enjoyed a decade of unprecedented growth. Turkey is now in a *prime position* to become an even more important ally to the U.S. given its *robust economy.*

As I describe in my recent monograph, The Rise of Turkey, the country has now become *a majority middle-class society.* This has yielded impressive results: Turkey is on the cusp of becoming the *first large Muslim majority society to attain universal literacy.* Economic development has connected the Turkish people to the rest of the world in ways that cannot be reversed.

Equally comforting are *improvements in terms of religious freedoms,* especially for non-Muslim communities. Property belonging to church and synagogue foundations, confiscated by the government in the 20th century, has been returned to their owners. Some historic sanctuaries closed since the end of the Ottoman Empire, such as the Greek-Orthodox Sumela Monastery and Gregorian Armenian Akdamar Church, have been re-opened for services. Artuklu University in southern Turkey teaches Hebrew as well as Syriac-Aramaic, the language that Jesus spoke.

Mr. Chairman, for these key *accomplishments,* Turkey's ruling Justice and Development Party (*AKP*) and its Prime Minister, Recep Tayyip *Erdogan,* deserve *credit.*

However, there is also a less bright side to the AKP's legacy. *Under the party, Turkey has become more prosperous, but ironically, at the same time, also less free.* When the party took power in 2002, Turkey's record on liberties, as measured by international indices, improved along with the country's ambitious work to qualify for European Union (EU) accession. Later under the AKP, Turkey's record on *liberties* stagnated, subsequently taking a *nose dive.*

For example, according to the Freedom House, in 2001 before the AKP, Turkey ranked 58 out of 100 in terms of press freedom: 100 being the least free and the 0 being the most free. In 2005, this score improved to 48. But later, it started to decline, dropping to 62 in 2013. Turkey under the AKP is worse off than before when it comes to freedoms.

Despite being elected through a democratic process, the AKP has governed in an *authoritarian* manner. The party has made habit of quashing any opposition, most prominently during the 2013 Gezi Park rallies where police used tear gas and water cannons on protesters. The recent Twitter and YouTube ban is the latest example of the AKP's propensity for curbing basic freedoms.

A second alarming issue concerning the U.S. has been Turkey's *pivot to the Middle East* which has *met serious challenges*. Before the AKP, the Turks thought of themselves as a European country situated next to the Middle East. Towards the end of the last decade, Ankara decided that the path to greater power and influence was through the Middle East rather than Europe.

This has turned out to be a miscalculation. With the exception of the Kurds, Turkey currently has *no allies in the Middle East*. What is more, the country is flanked by enemies, ranging from the Assad regime to "Islamic State" (IS), as well as brutal competitors such as Iran and Saudi Arabia.

Among the many problems with Turkey's Middle East policy IS poses the gravest threat. It wants to establish a Taliban-like state across Turkey's 800-mile-long border with Iraq and Syria. Nobody wants the Taliban as a neighbor or its presence in the Middle East. Ankara, Washington and NATO need each other to combat this threat. Mr. Chairman, this cooperation will *cement a strong U.S.-Turkey relationship* in years to come because *what is in Turkey's interest is in the United States' interest.*

The Turkish prime minister has a personal stake in eradicating IS as well. Mr. Erdogan wins elections because Turkey grows, and the country grows because it attracts international investment. Chaos next door will dry up money flowing to Turkey, ending Mr. Erdogan's successful run in the elections.

The emergence of IS offers green shoots even for the future of *Turkish-Israeli ties*. Surrounding Turkey to the south, IS has cut the country off from its Middle Eastern markets. To circumvent this, Turkish companies now ship their goods to the Israeli port of Haifa where Jordanian truck drivers take them across the Middle East, through Saudi Arabia, to the Persian Gulf. This has reminded the Turks of the need to cooperate with the Israelis, including on the eastern Mediterranean gas deposits, as well as in combatting IS.

Mr. Chairman, there are other reasons to be optimistic about Turkey's future: *the middle class*, which has grown as a result of the AKP's economic policies, is committed to individual freedoms and is now *challenging the party's style of governance.*

The main opposition *Republican People's Party (CHP) is slowly* but surely becoming a *liberal movement*. Recently, the State Department awarded party deputy Safak Pavey with International Woman of Courage Award, recognizing CHP's commitment to gender equality and democratic values.

Mr. Chairman, *Turkey's trajectory points toward democracy*, and makes its ascension into the EU an attractive prospect. For years, the Turks aspired to join the Union hoping it would make their country richer and more democratic. Turkey is already wealthy thanks to the AKP, and the lure of EU to attain prosperity is no longer there. But, as Europe needs Turkey as a buffer against Middle Eastern instability, the *Turkish people need the EU to drive further democratic reform at home.*

U.S. policy should *encourage* Turkish *reorientation towards Europe.* We stand at an opportune moment regarding such a pivot. The AKP's drive to transform Turkey into a Middle Eastern power has failed and the Turks feel burnt out from such efforts.

This became clearer when IS *attacked the Turkish consulate* in Mosul on June 11, taking 49 Turkish citizens, including children, hostage. To this date, Ankara has not been able to secure the release of its citizens. This is the largest hostage crisis in Turkey's history.

The IS threat has caused many Turks to clamor for the day when their country stayed out of the Middle East and looked to Europe. *Washington should capitalize* on this, relying on *Turkey in the fight against IS* while *promoting the country's repositioning towards Europe.*

Mr. Chairman, *a European Turkey is not only a U.S. interest, but also an interest of Mr. Erdogan.* Nearly 80 percent of the foreign investment that flows into Turkey, fueling Mr. Erdogan's electoral victories, comes from the EU. Europeans invest in Turkey because they believe Ankara will maintain its connections with the continent. Turkey's leaders surely appreciate the wisdom of their country's European vocation.

Failing to consolidate power in the Middle East, *Ankara needs to re-embrace the EU and its democratic values.* The Middle East may not have panned out the way it hoped, but Turkey can still be a major player, *a major European player.*

Mr. Chairman, Turkey is of vital interest to Europe, and in turn the U.S. *Its location and proclivity to capitalism and democracy make it an important ally.* The developments facing Europe and the Middle East may have pushed *Turkey* from the forefront of the news, but it *must not be forgotten. Washington and Ankara share interests and Turkey's path will have great strategic importance to the U.S.* in situations ranging from Ukraine to Iraq and Syria for years to come.

Thank you.

———————

Mr. ROHRABACHER. Thank you very much. Dr. Kanat?

STATEMENT OF KILIC KANAT, PH.D., NON–RESIDENT SCHOLAR, FOUNDATION FOR POLITICAL, ECONOMIC, AND SOCIAL RESEARCH (SETA)

Mr. KANAT. Thank you, Mr. Chairman. I am deeply honored to discuss Turkey with you, and I greatly appreciate the invitation to do so. And you have my statement. This is a summary of my statement.

Democratization in Turkey has been a long and challenging process. And despite some bumps and concerns, Turkey's track record with democratization and societal transformation demonstrates that there will not be a reversal from democracy that will drag Turkey back to authoritarianism.

There are a couple of reasons that Dr. Cagaptay also mentioned. One of them is that democracy has been made possible in the last 10 years in part due to the rise of the middle class whose demands center around a more inclusive and representative governance. This new and growing social class has opposed any top-down approach in politics and has challenged the political and social engineering of previous decades. The class is now almost 50 percent of the population and economic indicators demonstrate that it will continue to grow in the coming years. It will be unlikely for this group to cede any democratic gains in the coming years, thus preventing any political party or actor from bringing Turkey back to the illiberalism of previous decades.

Second and related to this, this middle class, especially its youth, is more integrated with the world today. There is a growing number of active social media users that connect and interact with other users worldwide. The political and social demands of these citizens are increasing as they become more exposed to other cultures and they have increasingly used social media to express those demands.

Third, despite some criticism, the Turkish Government itself also recognizes the structural problems in Turkish democracy, which have been partly the residuals of previous periods and need to be resolved. In his vision statement for the Presidential election, for example, Prime Minister Erdogan made democratization the first of his three pillars in his candidacy platform.

The prime minister's recent statement of condolence to the Armenian victims of the events of 1915 and apology to the Alawites for the Dersim events can also be considered as steps toward this direction. Furthermore, the current government has also realized that it is politically expedient to favor democracy. Every political reform that the government has promoted has increased the strength of the AK Party and contributed to its electoral victories; it doesn't seem likely for the AK Party to change this course in the coming future.

Lastly, the European Union integration process will continue to play an important role in Turkey's democratization. Despite the declining enthusiasm of the Turkish public, mostly because of the discouraging statements of some European leaders about Turkey's potential membership, the EU process is still considered the most significant foreign policy dimension of Turkish politics. In order to avoid any disruption in its political and economic relations, the Turkish Government and society will not allow its democratic standards to fall short of the Copenhagen Criteria.

Although Turkey seems to be on the right track for democratization, it still has some significant problems. Most of these challenges are structural ones which may require more time, energy and co-operation from other parties. One of the most significant challenge lies in the formation of democratic institutions that will protect the democratic achievements of previous decades. Particularly in Turkey, an independent, impartial and credible judiciary is needed to consolidate the process of democratization and strengthen the rule of law in the country.

The judiciary has always been a major political actor in Turkey, and as such the public trust in the judiciary has been lower than in other democratic states. Although the referendum and legal reforms brought some improvement, there are still major problems. The majority of Turkey citizens' opinion that recent events were an attempt to launch a coup via the judiciary demonstrates the depth of Turkish peoples' mistrust in that branch of government. If Turkey wishes to consolidate and improve its democracy, the judiciary must also heed its responsibility to be an impartial and independent body.

Moreover, the government in the last 10 years has implemented many reform packages; however, these half-fixes of rights are no longer sufficient to satisfy the wishes of Turkish people. Consequently, a democratic and civilian Constitution is necessary in order to guarantee freedoms and liberties in the country. Drafting the Constitution must be an inclusive and pluralistic process to be considered a valid social contract. It must equally address the concern of all citizens in Turkish society in regards to freedom of religion, media and expression.

Finally, Turkey must develop a more powerful opposition that has a democratic, inclusive and representative vision in order to harness the support of the new middle class so that it can push for further democratization in the country. If not, Turkey will continue to face the problem of a weak and not very credible opposition as it did in the 2011 and 2014 elections, where the main opposition parties failed to act as a viable alternative to the AK Party. On the one hand, this absence of an opposition leaves the AK Party as the only party in the political arena capable of producing policy. On the other hand, the failure of opposition parties fosters mistrust for the political parties in general in Turkey, which fuels increasing street politics.

In summary, Turkey's path to democratization has been a challenging and convoluted one. However, the country has undergone an irreversible transformation and the next step its leaders must take should be to the consolidate the country's democratic gains by building institution, drafting a civilian Constitution and responding to the democratic demands of a rapidly changing society. Thank you very much.

[The prepared statement of Mr. Kanat follows:]

DEMOCRACY IN TURKEY

Kilic Bugra Kanat

Penn State University, Erie
SETA Foundation, Washington, DC

Democratization in Turkey has been a long and challenging process. Since the first proper multiparty elections in 1950, the process of democratization in Turkey has been consistently interrupted by military coups and judicial interferences. For decades, the system of tutelage led by the Turkish military and judiciary controlled the political landscape and made decisions on which rights and liberties would be granted to Turkish society at large. In this tutelary system, the judiciary helped the military control the entry into politics and prosecuted politicians and intellectuals that challenged the premises of Kemalism. The military and the judiciary engineered the political system in the country, while the military-controlled media and "civil society organizations" tried to shape public opinion. This tutelage in Turkey created its own middle class of bureaucrats and a crony capitalist system where a small group of businessmen enjoyed special privileges. When the military considered this tutelary system insufficient or when the civilian political sphere was getting "out of control," it directly intervened in politics through military coups.

While the tutelary system aimed to allow only a minimal degree of democratization in the country, military coups attempted to eradicate the existing political system and design a new one that was conducive to the military's goals and principles, namely: preserving the state's Kemalist ideology and protecting it from its citizens, limiting the space for civil society, and excluding conservative Anatolians and Kurds from state institutions. For instance, after the 1980 coup, all political parties were banned in Turkey and all known political actors were prohibited from running for office. The military designed a new constitution that granted it more power and established institutions that would guarantee its continued influence after it transferred power to a civilian government. In fact, the transition to democracy was engineered in such a way that the military would have the final say in every step of the electoral process, including determining which political parties could participate, the candidates that could join the race and the content of campaigns.

The Ozal period represented one of the first attempts to liberalize the economy and the political sphere after decades of military tutelage. Despite rifts between the military and Ozal, the majority of his economic policies were implemented and Turkey witnessed significant changes to its social structure with the emergence of a new middle class. Later called the "Anatolian Tigers," this new class of businessmen, who mostly owned small and medium-sized enterprises in Central Anatolian cities, started to play a more active role in the economy and politics. While Ozal managed to liberalize the economy, he failed to achieve the same degree of liberalization in the political sphere. Despite some improvements in the freedom of expression and conscience, Turkey continued to have significant problems in terms of human rights and liberties. The emerging threat of the Kurdistan Workers' Party (PKK) and its activities exacerbated the domestic threat perception in Turkey, leading to the rise of the Kurdish problem and the failure to take meaningful steps to resolve it.

In the 1990s, the political structure formed by the military after the 1980 coup started to create major problems. Political deadlock and failed attempts to form coalition governments led to the emergence of a power vacuum, which was filled by the military and the bureaucracy. Different dynamics also started to emerge during this period. On the one hand, the Kurdish problem started to take the form of a low intensity conflict. The number of violent attacks by the PKK increased and the state reacted by using harsh political and military tactics. During this time, the Kurdish problem was equated with the PKK, while its sociological roots and causes were mostly ignored. On the other hand, the Turkish state started to perceive the rise of the Welfare Party and its conservative leader, Necmettin Erbakan, as well as an increasing effective conservative middle class, as major threats. Once again, the Kemalist establishment neglected the movement's sociological roots and the Welfare Party, as well as different religious and conservative networks, was equated with a fundamentalist organization that threatened Turkey's secularism, Western orientation and democracy. These threat perceptions led to major violations against human rights and freedom of expression and practices that would challenge the basic tenets of democracy in Turkey. While torture and unlawful detention became widespread, conservative segments of the society, especially women who wore headscarves, were not allowed to enter universities or work in the public sector; certain independent religious schools were also banned.

Both the conservative and Kurdish movements in Turkey were natural responses to the structure of the Kemalist state. For years, these actors were kept at the periphery at the expense of the urbanized, statist, educated, secular and Western center. This center-periphery dichotomy had three elements: a geographical dimension, as Kurds and more conservative segments of the society resided in the less urbanized regions of Turkey; a sociological dimension in which both of these groups were considered as the "other" by the Kemalist order; and an economic dimension, as the center was industrialized and educated and the periphery was underdeveloped and less educated. Demographically, the periphery represented the majority of society, while a minority controlled the center. In the 1970s, the geographical dimension of this structure was altered by migration from the countryside to cities. In the 1980s, the rising Anatolian middle class and PKK violence challenged the economic and security dimension of the center. This challenge became more visible during the 1990s, when the existing political system failed to meet the societal demands of a rising middle class and those of ethnic and religious groups.

The 1997 military intervention, known as the "post-modern coup," was another attempt by the military to design politics and "realign democracy." After the National Security Council (NSC), which was dominated by the military, released a memorandum, the media, civil society and business groups pressured the government to resign. The judiciary then launched its own campaign to close the Welfare Party. After the Welfare Party was shut down, a military solution to the Kurdish problem was prioritized. Turkey underwent a major democratic reversal after the military's intervention.

It was under these circumstances that the Justice and Development Party (AKP or AK Party) was formed and rose to power in 2002. The AK Party was brought to power largely due to the Anatolian middle class' increasing demands for a more inclusive and representative government, and society's frustration the existing political parties' inability to deal with the political and economic problems in the country. The AK Party's electoral victory, which came only a year after it was established, was also a social response to the military and judiciary tutelage that designed politics between 1997 and 2002.

The AK Party rose to power during a very significant juncture of Turkish politics. First of all, Turkey was recovering from the most devastating economic crisis in its history. The devaluation of the Turkish lira and the banking sector crisis, together with high inflation, crippled the Turkish economy in 2001. During the November 2002 elections, Turkey was still experiencing the after-effects of this crisis. Secondly, the 1997 military intervention and tutelary regime placed constraints on basic freedoms and liberties, which significantly lowered the standards of democracy in the country. Lastly, an external factor emerged with Turkey's European Union candidacy. After many years of negotiations, Turkey was accepted as an official candidate country to the EU and there was great enthusiasm to speed up the process. This was particularly challenging for the military in Turkey because the tutelary system had always considered Westernization as a source of legitimacy for its rule against the backward periphery. Now, Westernization necessitated democratic reforms that would challenge the military's authority in the country.

For the AK Party, the only way to overcome this impasse was to extend freedoms and liberties in the country in order to meet society's demands and guarantee a more secure political order. The European integration process was significant in allowing the party to pass important reform packages regarding the freedom of expression, thought and organization under the tutelary system. The AK Party government met the conditions to launch accession negotiations with the EU, which guarantee the rule of law, democracy, human rights and liberties. Meanwhile, the AK Party continued to exercise extreme discipline in public spending, reaching every stated budget target and managing the economic reforms that were outlined in the IMF standby agreements. During this period, the economy began to grow rapidly. The success of its economic reforms and political opening resulted in the AK party's victory in subsequent general and local elections. Economic success during this period enlarged the middle class, increasing its influence in politics.

However, the process of political reform was not a smooth one. The Turkish military made several attempts, which were later uncovered, to overthrow the AK Party government. Most significantly, in April 2007, the military posted a memorandum online in order to interfere with the presidential election process. In response, the government rebuked the military and called early elections in July 2007, resulting in another landslide victory for the AK Party and an increase in their portion of the seats in the parliament. The election results openly demonstrated society's reaction to the military's intervention in politics.

The end of military tutelage and active civilian control over the military was one of the most significant achievements of the democratization process under the AK Party's rule. However, this did not completely end the system of tutelage. In 2008, the AK Party faced the judicial tutelage. The Prosecutor General in Turkey launched a lawsuit to close the AK Party and ban its leadership from running for office based on the charge of being the focal point of anti-secular activities. The Turkish judiciary has always been a very influential player in the continuation of the system of tutelage and has shut down many political parties in the past. This time, the Constitutional Court decided against closing down the AK Party by just one vote.

The AK Party responded to these attempts by launching a new reform process that brought important amendments to the constitution, including: a) eliminating the articles that provided protection for coup leaders; b) the right to collective bargaining for government employees; c) changes regarding the election of the members of the Constitutional Court and Higher Council of Judges and Prosecutors; and d) the right of individuals to file a petition to the Constitutional Court. The opposition parties did not agree with these amendments and voted against the reforms in parliament. In 2010, in order to institute these constitutional changes, the AK Party called for a popular referendum to decide on the constitutional reform package. After a hotly contested referendum, nearly 58 percent of the electorate voted for the judicial reforms. The opposition parties actively campaigned against these amendments.

Following the 2011 general elections, the Turkish government launched another reform process, which aimed to resolve one of the historical problems of Turkish politics: the Kurdish insurgency. Even in its first party platform in 2001, the AK Party expressed a willingness to depart from the mainstream approach to the Kurdish problem by recognizing the cultural differences and ideational dimension of the problem. This was a clear difference from the mainstream approach, which recognized the issue solely as a security/terror problem caused by economic underdevelopment in the region. However, during its first term in the government, the AK Party avoided confronting the problem mainly because of the possible reaction of the military. Later, in 2009, the Turkish government launched a Kurdish language TV channel and Kurdish language and literature departments were established in universities. Finally, after 2011, the resolution process was launched in order to resolve the Kurdish problem peacefully in Turkey. If both sides succeed in negotiating terms, implementing them and saving the process from potential spoilers, the development will be very instrumental in the democratization of Turkey and the increasing rights and liberties of the minorities in the country.

Turkish government has faced significant crises on its path to democratization since the 2011 general elections.. First, the Gezi Park protests that took place June 2013 created a major crisis in Turkey. Despite several attempts by the administration to calm the demonstrators, the protests turned into anti-government rallies, propelled forward with the involvement of opposition parties and marginal leftist groups. Some of these groups even attempted to break in to the prime minister's offices in Istanbul and Ankara. A few months after the protests, the government faced a politically motivated corruption scandal that centered around the release of controversial government tapes. The release of one such tape leaked sensitive discussions of foreign policy in Syria among Turkish Foreign Minister Davutoglu, intelligence chief Hakan Fidan and the Army's deputy chief of staff; by releasing such sensitive information, what was a mere political move turned into a matter of national security. Both of these crises slowed down the democratization and reforms of Turkey.

The Future?

Despite concerns regarding the status of democratization in Turkey, the track record of the AK Party as well as the social and political changes Turkey has undergone indicate that there will not be a democratic reversal that will bring Turkey back to authoritarianism.

First, what has made democratization possible in the last ten years has in part been the rise of a middle class that demands more inclusive and representative governance in Turkey. This new and growing social class has opposed any top-down approach in government and has challenged the political and social engineering of previous decades. This class now is almost 50 percent of population in Turkey. According to economic forecasts, this middle class will only continue to grow in the coming years and will continue to wield influence over Turkish politics. If this class believes that the AK Party cannot meet their political and economic demands, it will most likely look to another party that can. Therefore, this social class will vocally assert its needs and keep Turkey from regressing into an illiberal democracy or authoritarianism.

Second, rapid economic growth in Turkey has also created a more educated youth that is globally integrated, particularly due to their use of social media. This demographic is less homogenous culturally and more cosmopolitan than previous generations. The broad-based use of technology among this group makes it possible for the youth to mobilize effectively against the policies they deem not democratic. This youth and their mobilization is impossible for political parties in a democracy to ignore. The demands of these youth are also growing and will be extremely influential in shaping the future trajectory of the Turkish democracy. It is again highly unlikely for this youth to allow the emergence of a more authoritarian Turkey in the future.

Third, the AK Party government has also recognized the structural problems in Turkish democracy and signaled that it will act in order to improve the current system. Statements by Turkish ministers in recent months, including the latest vision statement by PM Erdogan, indicate that there will be a major reform package after the presidential elections in August. PM Erdogan has even made democratization one of the three pillars of his presidential political platform and has constantly referred the concept of an "open society." Erdogan's speech has also signaled a more pluralistic approach to democracy that will recognize cultural, ethnic and religious differences in the country as well as equal citizenship rights for everyone.

The AK Party's track record over the last ten years demonstrates that its eagerness to address the most significant problems in Turkish democracy, including the Kurdish question and the military's intervention in politics. The party's devotion is made clear in its recent statement of condolences to the Armenian community for the events of 1915 as well as in its apology to Alawites for the events in Dersim in the 1930s. Furthermore, the current government has also realized that it is politically expedient to favor democracy; every political reform the government has promoted has increased the strength of the AK Party and contributed to its electoral victories. Even if solely for its self-interest, the AK Party government would continue to promote Turkey's democratization.

Lastly, the EU integration process will continue to play an important role in Turkey's domestic politics and democratization in the coming decades. Despite the declining enthusiasm of the Turkish public, mostly due to the discouraging statements made by European leaders regarding Turkey's potential membership, the EU process is still considered the most significant foreign policy dimension of Turkish politics. The EU is Turkey's largest trading partner and will remain so for the near future. In order to avoid any disruption of its political and economic relations, the Turkish government and society will not allow its democratic standards to fall short of the Copenhagen Criteria and the EU acquis.

In the coming years, there are some important challenges that need to be addressed by the government in order to improve Turkey's democratic standards. However, most of these challenges are structural ones, which may require more time and energy and necessitate the contribution of other parties. One of the most significant is the formation of democratic institutions that will protect past democratic achievements. Institution-building should be considered a major dimension of democratic consolidation, alongside political will and societal demands for democratization. As demonstrated by recent events in Turkey, an independent, impartial and credible judiciary is needed to consolidate the process of democratization and strengthen the rule of law. The judiciary has always been a major political actor in Turkey, and until recently, it was considered as another pillar of tutelage that was responsible for the protection of the state ideology. The referendum and legal reforms in Turkey alleviated part of this problem, but left others, such as the question of impartiality, unsolved. Therefore, public trust of the judiciary is lower in Turkey compared to other democratic states. The fact that recent events were considered an attempted judicial coup by the majority of Turkish society demonstrates how people in Turkey perceive the role of the judiciary. If Turkey wants to consolidate its democracy and achieve higher standards in this realm, the judiciary needs to exercise judicial prudence and gain the status of an impartial and independent body.

Second, various attempts to amend the current constitution demonstrated that it would be easier to pursue democratization with a new and civilian constitution. In the last ten years, the government has proposed different reform packages and multiple changes to the constitution. However, partial improvements on democratic principles and human rights within the current constitution may no longer be sufficient to meet the desired democratic standards. A new civilian, pluralistic, and democratic constitution is needed. The process of drafting of this new constitution needs to be inclusive and pluralistic and respond to the demands of different segments of Turkish society.

Third, Turkey also needs a more powerful opposition that can connect with the middle class with a more democratic, inclusive and representative vision. The 2011 general elections and the 2014 local elections demonstrate that Turkish democracy suffers from the lack of a credible opposition. The main opposition parties failed to present a new and democratic perspective and become a viable alternative to the AK Party. The opposition's inability to creatively address national issues transformed these parties by restricting their bases to only certain regions, while their support evaporated in others. While this situation renders the AK Party as the only party that can produce policies, it creates mistrust among political parties in the anti-AK Party camp, which fuels street politics.

Another important challenge is the necessity of balancing freedom and national security. The fact that two of Turkey's neighbors are in the midst of a civil war that may have spillover effects and the fact that Turkey was vulnerable to espionage activities, which was revealed in recent leaks, demonstrate that Turkey will have to take steps in the coming months to strengthen its national security. However, these steps needs to be taken in such a way that it will not challenge basic freedoms and liberties in the country. We have had this debate in the U.S. for the last fifteen years and we know that the delicate balance between freedom and security may be difficult to handle in certain instances.

To sum up, the democratization process in Turkey has been a long and convoluted one. Democratization has also been a moving target in Turkey, as the growing middle class and globally integrated youth are always coming up with new demands. When you take into account the residue of decades of illiberal politics in Turkey, and the actors and institutions of a tutelary regime that resist democratization, it becomes clear that there may be challenging episodes ahead. However, as mentioned above, when societal demands for these rights combine with political will, the system enters into an irreversible path towards democratization. As Turkey has already entered an irreversible trajectory, the next steps need to be towards democratic consolidation through institution-building, a civilian, democratic and pluralistic constitution, and a government that can respond to the new demands of a transforming society that is connected to the rapidly changing global system.

———

Mr. ROHRABACHER. Thank you very much, and next we have Mr. Tasci.

STATEMENT OF MR. HAKAN TASCI, EXECUTIVE DIRECTOR, TUSKON–US

Mr. TASCI. Thank you, Mr. Chairman and members of the committee, for giving me the opportunity to testify on the future of Turkish democracy. The following is summary of my prepared remarks. And I am a little bit sick, so I am sorry about that.

The AKP government transformed Turkey into an upper middle income country with a strong middle class and more than 20 powerhouse Anatolian cities in last decade. In order to overcome the middle income trap, however, structural reforms are essential and, specifically, tax code, institutional structure and the judicial system. Turkey's growth model is dependent on capital flows, foreign energy resources and Central Bank policies, especially before the municipal elections, they successfully controlled the exchange rate 3:40:00 in Turkey. And the independence of the Central Bank, which is increasingly undermined by Mr. Erdogan during the process, has been a key factor for combating inflation and financial stability.

Other investor worries are the problem with rule of law, diminishing economy and political checks and balances. Having tamed the military and crushed political opposition, Mr. Erdogan consolidated his power by suppressing the media and dissent to a large extent. This disproportional use of force and harsh rhetoric against Gezi Park protestors sparked an outcry inside Turkey and abroad. Mr. Erdogan has presented events as an international conspiracy to undermine his government and portrayed dissenters as traitors.

A similar pattern was evident during the corruption scandal of last December which implicated sons of three Turkish cabinet ministers, high level bureaucrats and government friendly businesses. Among the suspects are Reza Sarraf, an Iranian businessman dealing with gold trade in sanction era, and Yasin Al Qadi, a businessman who used to be on U.N. terror list for 10 years. Instead of complying with prosecutors, Mr. Erdogan presented corruption investigations as a coup effort led by domestic and international actors such as U.S. Ambassador, influential preacher Fethullah Gulen, and the ''interest lobby.''

In a clear attempt to obstruct justice, thousands of police officers and hundreds of prosecutors have been purged or reassigned. Turkish Parliament dominated by ruling party passed legislation which seriously threaten independence of judiciary and provides almost immunity to intelligence. This is a huge setback for rule of law and accountability in Turkey and quite antidemocratic laws.

Mr. Erdogan launched a fierce campaign against the Gulen movement, a major independent social force for democracy and modernization in Turkey, blaming it for masterminding the corruption investigations with the help of sympathizers in the bureaucracy. Pro-government media follows with orchestrated headlines and lies. The PM is not shy of publicly declaring this a witch hunt. Thousands of bureaucrats were discredited, demoted or reassigned. Without any evidence of wrongdoing, guilt by association has become the norm.

Witch hunt has taken a toll not only in bureaucracy but also in civil society, business community and media. He calls Gulen movement sympathizers in public mass as viruses, assassins, leeches, traitors, spies and vampires. In addition he is cancelling public tenders, changing zoning of existing structures——

Mr. CONNOLLY. Mr. Chairman, was he talking about Fox News? No, no.

Mr. TASCI. Cancelling public tenders, changing zoning of existing structures, revoking mining permits, deploying tax inspectors, rejecting venue rentals for programs are among the common practices. Members of my organization, TUSKON, a leading business NGO, face government retribution if they don't resign from membership. Bank Asya was nearly bankrupt due to orchestrated defunding efforts by the government.

Without any indictment or charge, Mr. Erdogan presses the U.S. Government to extradite Mr. Gulen who lives in Pennsylvania as a legal resident. White House had to issue a rare correction after he suggested that Mr. Obama agreed to comply with him. Media affiliated with the movement that maintains its independence is a constant target. Private tutoring centers will be closed starting June 2015 because of 25 percent stake of movement. Erdogan government heavily lobbies against the movement's peaceful and successful educational institutions in more than 150 nations, and some closed already due to pressure.

Undermining peaceful and constructive Sufi initiatives which offer an antidote to extremism and violence is a disservice not only to Turkey but to the world. Witch hunt and smear tactics is not limited to Gulen circles. Businessmen, associations and media who come from different ideological backgrounds are under intense pressure to either comply or face consequences. According to press reports, 100,000 small and midsized businesses were profiled based on their donations, flight arrangements and other confidential data.

AKP leadership tries to justify recent antidemocratic practices pointing out electoral victories. However, Professor Omer Taspinar describes this overturn as transformation from tyranny of Kemalist minority to "tyranny of majority." Prime Minister Erdogan thinks his election victory with 43 percent in March 30 municipal elections have cleared him and his party associates from the corruption allegations as well. He does not hide his ambition to force constitutional boundaries to make executive and legislative branches, if not judiciary, subservient to him.

And one last thing. The Erdogan government deserves credit with its continued commitment to resolution of the Kurdish question. And finally, Turkey is a strategically important country for the West as a relatively successful democractic and free market experiment in a volatile region. Turkey's Sufi interpretations of Islam represent a powerful alternative to violent extremism. Therefore it is imperative for friends and allies of Turkey in the West to support and engage Turkey on its democratic and economic journey.

Turkey's continued EU accession path is essential for reforms. TTIP, Transatlantic Trade and Investment Partnership, might open a new and an important gateway for Turkey's future integration with the EU and the U.S. One must not lose hope with the future of Turkey democracy and economic potential. Despite occasional downturns, Turkey has historically always found a way to recover.

[The prepared statement of Mr. Tasci follows:]

Statement of Hakan Taşçı
Executive Director, TUSKON US
Confederation of Businessmen and Industrialists of Turkey

Testimony Before the House Committee on Foreign Affairs
Subcommittee on Europe, Eurasia, and Emerging Threats:
"The Future of Turkish Democracy"
Tuesday, July 15, 2014

Two severe economic crises with the collapse of the banking system in 2001, led to an economic and political transformation in Turkey. Thanks to single party rule, EU-bound reform agendas, strong partnership with the IMF, and independent local agencies like the Central Bank Turkey successfully tamed inflation from 60% to single digits and public debt from 95 percent of GDP to 35 percent of GDP levels while tripling GDP. This success released billions of dollars spent on interest, which the government used. Generous healthcare reforms, social policies that funneled lots of money to low income households, high growth infrastructure projects and flexible land development led to procurement policies that generated high growth, new jobs and a successful economic outcome. Even the global financial crisis was weathered successfully thanks to the sound fiscal and monetary policy management and strong banking system. New infrastructure generates a strong Anatolian middle class and powerhouses all around the country.

However, nowadays after becoming an upper middle-income country reaching up to 11 thousand dollars per capital income levels with more than 20 powerhouse cities in Anatolia, Turkey is facing a middle-income trap. Structural reforms are essential in specifically tax code; institutional structure and the judicial system. Most of the local investments are devoted to real estate and construction, which can generate problems over the long term. A more export and innovation driven economy must be encouraged.

The Turkish economy needs around 55 billion dollars in annual international funds to close its current account deficit. Government debt (35% of GDP) is quite low so there is not that much of a problem there, however the private sector debt is worrisome. Turkish corporate debt is, around 60 percent of total assets, one of the highest among emerging economies. That's why companies and contractors responsible for major infrastructure projects are facing financing issues. In order to solve the problems of the government friendly contractors, even more preferential treatments such as government guarantees, tax amnesty are awarded to those friendly businesses. In a potential mismanagement, the government guarantees all of the losses, which can generate big burdens on the budget in the future.

Preferential and biased approach to business community is limiting new investments in the country. Institutional and transparent structures are undermined while personal treatment and leadership connectedness have become widespread to work with the government. Public tenders and land development requires the Prime Minister's (PM) direct approval. At the expense of meritocracy, clientalism and crony, capitalism is on the rise. The PM micromanages to such extent that he often personally decides who is going to build what and where.

The Federal Reserve is coming to an end in its quantitative easing and expansionary policies. Turkey like other emerging economies is affected from this trend. Recent exchange rate depreciation and the interest rate hike decision of the Central Bank in January 2014 eased the immediate effects. However, some of the ruling party officials' interventionist attitude may hamper the independence of the Central Bank having a detrimental effect on the economy in the long run. It is good to see that the economy management team generally understands the concerns.

Turkey's growth model is heavily dependent on the international capital flows and foreign energy resources. Policy makers need to put the current account deficit back on track to a downward trend, which already started after significant depreciation in the Turkish Lira, and control inflation as well as credit growth. Energy policies will have to focus on more renewable resources and alternative sources like Azeri and Iraqi gas and more transparent licensing system to encourage more investment. Regional crises in Iraq and Syria presents big trade challenges for the Turkish economy.

Another worry of investors is the problems with rule of law and erosion of economic and political checks and balances. Emboldened by 58 percent vote in 2010 referendum for constitutional amendments and 49 percent general elections victory in 2011, PM Erdoğan opted for the monopolization of power instead of continuing with the EU-bound reform agendas. Having tamed the military and crushed political opposition, he consolidated his power by suppressing media and dissent. His authoritarian tendencies were first evident with the disproportional use of force and harsh rhetoric against Gezi Park protesters in June 2013, which sparked an outcry inside Turkey and abroad. Mr. Erdoğan has presented Gezi events as an international conspiracy to undermine his government and portrayed dissenters as traitors.

A similar pattern was observed during the corruption scandal of last December which implicated sons of three Turkish cabinet ministers, high level bureaucrats and government friendly businessmen. Among the suspects are Reza Sarraf, a 29 year old Iranian businessmen dealing with Gold trade and Yasin Al Qadi, a businessman who used to be on the UN terror list for ten years due to his connections with Al Qaeda affiliates.

Instead of complying with prosecutors, Mr. Erdoğan presented the investigations as a political conspiracy led by domestic and international actors such as U.S. ambassador Francis Ricciardone, influential preacher Fethullah Gülen, *Wall Street Journal*, BBC and the "interest lobby." In a clear attempt to obstruct justice, thousands of police officers and hundreds of prosecutors were purged. Subsequently, Turkish parliament dominated by the ruling AKP, passed legislations which seriously threaten the independence of the judiciary. Since the AKP has tight control of both the executive and legislative branches, it is highly unlikely that members of the cabinet and parliament implicated by the corruption scandal will be impeached. This would be a huge setback for rule of law and government accountability in Turkey.

Due to government pressure and intimidation of the independent media, the Turkish nation was kept considerably in the dark about some of the crucial details of the corruption scandal. In order to hide the inconvenient truth from the people, YouTube and Twitter were banned until overruled by the Constitutional Court. It takes real courage for media organizations to run stories on corruption scandals or question government actions on any other topic. The Prime minister personally chastises media bosses and intervenes in on the editorial process. Those who do not comply are subjected to smear campaigns by government and pro-government media. Media owners either have to fire journalists or face the consequences like Akın Ipek, the owner of Bugün newspaper and Kanaltürk television. As an apparent retaliation to the coverage of the corruption scandal by his media, the government revoked three mine licenses of Mr. Ipek. The chairman of TUSIAD, one of the largest business associations in Turkey, was declared a 'traitor' after he said a country cannot draw foreign investment when there is no respect for the rule of law. He faced pressures to keep quiet and finally had to quit from his job citing his business problems. Ambassador James Holmes, CEO and President of the American Turkish Council, a prominent DC based non-profit business organization had to offer his resignation due to pressure from the Erdoğan government and government friendly businessmen.

Lately, at the epicenter of Prime Minister Erdoğan's conspiracy theories, smears and discriminatory practices is Hizmet (a.k.a Gülen movement). The Gülen Movement is a transnational faith-inspired civic movement arising in Turkey during the late 1960s. Inspired by prominent religious scholar Fethullah Gülen's peaceful ideas and dedicated to the traditional Turkish Sufi tenets of modesty, mutual understanding, respect, spirituality, and intellectual enlightenment, Hizmet (means 'The Service' in English) appeals to people from diverse backgrounds. Participants of the movement have been active in all walks of life including education, business, media and relief. They run successful private schools in Turkey and more than 150 countries focusing on science and foreign languages. With its anti-violent, globalization friendly, pro-EU-accession, pro-democracy and nonconfrontational outlook, The Gülen movement offers an antidote to political and radical interpretations of Islam.

Although until recently many sympathizers of the movement have voted for the AK Party due to a lack of credible alternatives, there has always been underlying differences between the two groups. Prime Minister Erdoğan's ambition to design and subordinate civil society has exacerbated tension between the government and independent groups such as the Gülen movement. Mr. Erdoğan has started to question the loyalty of Gülen movement sympathizers to him and his party in bureaucracy as well. With those prejudices in mind, he was quick in blaming Mr. Gülen and his movement for staging a 'coup' plots against the Erdoğan government with corruption investigations. PM Erdoğan was not shy of publicly admitting his antidemocratic actions against the Gülen movement tantamount to a "witch hunt". Thousands of bureaucrats from various government offices were discredited, demoted or reassigned due to perceived ties or sympathies with the Gülen movement. Guilt by association has become the norm, however no single wrongdoing has been legally proven so far. Mr. Erdoğan also presses the US government to extradite Mr. Gülen who lives in Pennsylvania as a legal resident without any indictment, court case or charge. The White House had to issue a rare correction after he suggested that Mr. Obama agreed to comply with his unlawful requests. Mr. Erdoğan's inflammatory rhetoric includes calling Gülen movement sympathizers viruses, assassins, leeches, traitors, spies, and vampires. Media affiliated with the Hizmet movement that maintains its independence has also been a constant target.

Witch-hunt has taken a toll not only in bureaucracy but also in civil society, business community, and media. Canceling public tenders, rezoning existing structures, revoking business permits, deploying tax inspectors are among the common practices. Members of TUSKON, a leading business NGO, face government retribution if they don't resign from membership. Bank Asya was nearly bankrupt due to orchestrated defunding efforts by the government. Private tutoring centers for the national student placement exams will be closed starting June 2015 because of the 25 percent stake of the Gülen movement in the sector. The Erdoğan government heavily lobbies against the movement's educational institutions abroad. Several countries had to comply not to lose their investments in Turkey. Despite court orders, pro-government news outlets continue running fabricated stories about the Gülen movement on a daily basis.

The Erdoğan government's controversial tactics are not limited to Gülen circles. Businessmen, associations and media who come from different ideological backgrounds are under intense pressure to either comply or face consequences. According to press reports, one hundred thousand small and mid-size businesses were profiled based on their donations, flight arrangements and other private data.

AKP leadership tries to justify recent anti-democratic practices pointing out to their electoral victories. However NDU Professor and Brookings scholar Dr. Ömer Taşpınar describes this overturn as transformation from the tyranny of Kemalist minority to 'tyranny of majority'. PM Erdoğan thinks his election victory with 43% percent during the March 30 municipal elections in the immediate aftermath of the corruption scandal, has cleared him and his party associates of corruption allegations as well. He now runs for presidency and does not hide his ambitions to use his constitutional powers in a way that will make executive and legislative branches, if not judiciary, subservient to him if he wins. Both opposition candidates, Prof. Ekmeleddin Ihsanoğlu and Mr. Selahattin Demirtaş, reject the notion that Turkey would be better off with a de-facto presidential system without necessary checks and balances as Mr. Erdoğan suggests. Many observers think establishing a one man rule and a party state in Turkey would compound political and societal tensions leading to instability.

Despite generally negative trends in freedoms and democracy in the last few years, Turkish government deserves credit for its continued commitment to the resolution of Kurdish question. Prime Minister Erdoğan has spent a considerable amount of his political capital on negotiations with leadership of the PKK, a terrorist organization, including Abdullah Öcalan who is serving a life sentence in a Turkish prison. Whether or not both sides will eventually make serious concessions on political and security grounds remains to be seen. Critics claim Erdoğan might abandon nationalist Kurds after he garners their votes in the presidential elections. In that case, a return to armed conflict which cost Turkey more than 30,000 lives over three decades might be inevitable.

Despite improvements, reports by international and domestic human rights groups still point out to continued problems for Turkey's religious and ethnic minorities, women, media and others. Alevis, Kurds, Christians seek more rights. The mother of many lingering rights issues is the 1982 Turkish Constitution enacted at a post-military-coup period. There is a consensus on changing the Constitution but not an agreement on how to do it. Polarization in politics and society also doesn't help.

All that said, one must not lose hope or optimism with the future of Turkish democracy. Despite occasional downturns, Turkey has historically found ways to recover and improve. Turkey is a relatively successful democratic and free market experiment in a volatile but strategically important region. Turkish Sufi interpretations of Islam represent a powerful alternative to violent extremism. Hence it's imperative for friends and allies of Turkey in the West to support and engage with Turkey on its democratic and economic journey. As one of the major intellectual forums in Turkey, Abant Platform has recently declared, Turkey's continued EU accession path as essential for reforms. On the economic front, making Turkey part of the Transatlantic Trade and Investment Partnership (TTIP) process might open a new and an important gateway for anchoring

Turkey to the West. Turkey's value as a security partner in NATO can only be reinforced by further economic integration with EU and US.

In his latest book 'Why Nations Fail?' MIT Professor Daron Acemoğlu emphasizes the importance of the institutions, rule of law, freedoms and their effect on the sustainable development of the nations. Enhanced democracy with free press, flourishing civil society and independent courts also ensure a powerful economy. Therefore, Turkey's leaders and international friends should never waver on supporting and investing on Turkey's democratic and economic success, which goes hand in hand.

———

Mr. ROHRABACHER. Thank you very much.

Mr. Connolly, with the permission of the committee and unless I hear any objections, Mr. Connolly will be treated as a member of the committee.

Mr. CONNOLLY. I thank my friend.

Mr. ROHRABACHER. All right. Well, let me just ask, well, first of all, let me just note I accept that there is criticism and just criticism of Turkey or any other country. What we need to do is make sure that that criticism is within the perspective of what is happening in other countries and what is the norm and whether Turkey is operating as a norm or whether or not Turkey is headed in the wrong direction which is not the norm.

And let me just go through a few things here. You were mentioning about, Doctor, what was going on in Cyprus. Although this is not a hearing on Cyprus, this is a hearing on democracy in Turkey, are there mosques in the Christian areas that have not been, and property in the Christian areas of Cyprus that are also being— your criticism of how the Christian churches and properties are being treated in the Muslim side of Cyprus, what about in the other areas? Is there a balance there somewhere, or the Turkey side is way more repressive against Christians than the Christian side is against Muslims?

Ms. PRODROMOU. The only reason that I introduced what was happening in Turkish occupied Cyprus was because I think it is a very useful metric for the overall quality of democracy in Turkey. After all, the Turkish Armed Forces have absolute control over the northern part of Cyprus and unfortunately there is a pattern in the occupied section of Cyprus that I think speaks to the broader pattern in terms of what has happened with religious freedom issues on the Turkish mainland.

Mr. ROHRABACHER. To be specific, the specific question I asked is your testimony criticized the activities going on in the Turkish areas with Christian properties. Can that same criticism be leveled in Christian areas to Islamic properties?

Ms. PRODROMOU. Absolutely not.

Mr. ROHRABACHER. Okay, good. That is what I am looking for. Because we had a bill about return of Christian properties. And by the way I am in favor of return of properties to people who they belong to whether they are Christians or Muslims. But there was a hearing that we had and I have also heard that there are Muslim properties in mosques in Greece, for example, that needed to be addressed as well.

And what we need to hear and what we need to find out, is it a just criticism of Turkey alone? We as a people who believe in freedom and treating people decently would hope no countries participate in this, but also we have to make sure we are not singling out one country for criticism that is of activities that are going on in all countries.

Let me ask about the censorship there. And at this time is the Internet censored in Turkey?

Mr. SCHENKKAN. It is a complicated question. There are upwards of, I believe the number is upwards of 30,000 Internet sites that are blocked——

Mr. ROHRABACHER. Blocked?

Mr. SCHENKKAN [continuing]. In Turkey. Blocked.

Mr. ROHRABACHER. So blocked by whom?

Mr. SCHENKKAN. Blocked by the government. Blocked by the telecommunications.

Mr. ROHRABACHER. So we have 30,000 sites that are blocked by the government.

Mr. SCHENKKAN. That is correct. And that includes sites that a democracy might also recognize as——

Mr. ROHRABACHER. Like pornography, gambling.

Mr. SCHENKKAN. There could be legitimate reasons for blocking sites. The question is whether——

Mr. ROHRABACHER. How many of them are? How many would you say are——

Mr. SCHENKKAN. We don't know because the government doesn't release a list of sites. This number is gathered by an NGO. The government stopped releasing a list, I think it was 3 years ago.

Mr. ROHRABACHER. Well, we have a testimony from this witness that says that the government is relying on social media to promote progress in their country. And we have another testimony here saying that we are blocking all of these sites but we don't know whether or not how many of them are political or they may be very legitimate blockage.

Mr. SCHENKKAN. Well, what we can say is that the process for blocking sites is not transparent. It is not able to be contested by the owners or the users of the site, and has been the subject of European Court of Human Rights ruling on this issue, a 2012 ruling, Yildirim v. Turkey, which held that the law that I mentioned that was amended, in my remarks, 5651, that this law was not in line with the European Convention on Human Rights which is legally binding upon Turkey. And the court said that Turkey needed to revise that law. They did not do so. They made these amendments this year that actually made the problems worse.

Mr. ROHRABACHER. Okay, well, let me get to the—you have mentioned again the judicial activity involved with some of these questions. One of our witnesses talked about the purge, the purge of judiciary. All right. But we heard from another witness that traditionally Turkish judiciary is political and politicized. So it is a purge to kick out certain people of a political persuasion when they themselves took the spot of someone because they were more in tune with that political persuasion? So is that a justified criticism then? I will give you a chance to answer that.

Mr. TASCI. I can say a few words on it. I mean as I said in the beginning of my remarks, the judicial system was always a problem in Turkey. It didn't start on December 17th or during the Gezi protest or even before. But the problem is the people who are not a problem on December 16th become the problem within the judicial system on December 17th, which happens. I mean what happened in that period, just 2 days after the December 17 investigations is filed, they said this is very big case and appointed two new prosecutors to the system, now three. And two of those three signed the prisonment (sic) of the suspects. Then those two were again purged, 3 or 4 days after the election.

So this is not about the politics of the judiciary or impartial behavior of the judiciary, as it becomes an are you with me or are you against me? Are you going to follow what I say?

Mr. ROHRABACHER. That leads to the question that I have got to lead up to here, and that is we have—look, we are Americans and demand a certain standard. And let me just say that I am not in favor of our Government getting involved in the Internet at all. I am for Internet freedom. But right now we are trying to assess democracy in Turkey, all right. And if indeed we have seen this type of politicization of the judiciary in the past as standard, to criticize Turkey right now on that is not necessarily a just criticism of this administration.

Now with that said, I am going to let my colleagues have their chance, but I would like to get a one answer from all of you. And that is, with the challenges or the problems that we are talking about right now this is, Turkey seems to be stepping back from the positive direction in democracy, et cetera that we had all been so happy about 10 years ago and 5 years ago, is this a problem with structure? The judiciary has always been politicized. Or is it a problem with you have got a leader with an ego who is now exercising powers that because of his own personal evaluation it is more of a personal thing? Because this happens to leaders around the world as well, I might add, that if they stay in too long—that is why George Washington stepped forward and said he is getting out after 8 years by the way and George Washington saved our country a lot of anguish because of that. Maybe after 8 years people begin to lose the perspective when they have had so much power. So is it structural or is it personal? Just give me, what is it?

Mr. SCHENKKAN. Both.

Mr. ROHRABACHER. Both, okay.

Doctor?

Ms. PRODROMOU. It is both, but I think it is more deeply structural than personal.

Mr. ROHRABACHER. Okay.

Mr. CAGAPTAY. I think it is structural but that is not the reason it should stay around. The argument that you always had problems with judiciary and media freedoms in Turkey, therefore problems today should be recognized is anachronistic. Turkey is a European country. It should have European style liberties. And justifying violations of freedom of expression based on past violations is not an excuse.

Mr. ROHRABACHER. Let me just note, I never justify any violation of human rights.

Mr. CAGAPTAY. I didn't suggest——

Mr. ROHRABACHER. I know, but I accept that as the standard that you are mentioning there.

Yes, sir?

Mr. KANAT. I think it is mainly structural.

Mr. ROHRABACHER. Structural.

Mr. TASCI. I think both.

Mr. ROHRABACHER. Both. Oh my. Well, thank you very much. I will now turn to our ranking member.

Mr. KEATING. Thank you, Mr. Chairman. Mention that Turkey's in a very dangerous neighborhood, and we are all saddened by the news of the Turkish hostages in Mosul and urge that they are released quickly. But this really poses a question in my mind because there have been other reports that the Turkish Government aids extremist factions in Syria, maybe not militarily but with access to borders and medical help and other types of help.

So how do you reconcile this that in one sense the government has been doing this, reports are indicating, while falling victim to the groups themselves. Are the reports accurate? What would ISIS particularly target in Turkey? Why would they do that if they were getting this kind of help? And how are the Turkish people hearing about this given some of the blackouts in communication that occur?

So I just wanted to get into that and I would like to ask Dr. Cagaptay first and then Dr. Kanat.

Mr. CAGAPTAY. Thank you, Congressman. I think for a long time Turkish-Syria policy was based on the following premise, Assad will fall and good guys will take over, therefore anyone who wants to go in and fight Assad can do so because when the good guys take over they will just sweep them away. That premise has proven to be wrong, and just as other premises of Turkey's pivot to the Middle East have produced problematic results.

Assad is not falling and good guys are not taking over, so the policy of letting anyone and everyone go in is creating threats long and short term for Turkey. And I think Turkey is now coming to grips with this conclusion that not only good guys are not taking over, but bad guys are laying roots in Syria. And ISIS attack on Turkey was unfortunate and rude wake-up call for many Turks who did not realize that this group had built an infrastructure in Syria, just as it was a rude wake-up call for us here in Washington.

I think at this stage, Turkey having come to this realization, this actually puts Turkey and the United States on an alignment. Now Turkey does see a radicalization threat coming from Syria which has targeted Turkey. ISIS when it took over Mosul, also attacked the Turkish consulate in that city, took 49 Turkish citizens including children and babies hostage, and to this day Turkey has not been able to secure their release. This is the worst hostage crisis in Turkey's modern history, and the threat comes from a radical group next door, ISIS that has grown in Syria.

To me this suggests an even closer U.S.-Turkish cooperation on Syria on the issue of radicalization because now ISIS is as big a threat to Turkey as it is to any other country in the region.

Mr. KEATING. And is that sifted down to the people?

Mr. CAGAPTAY. Yes, I have seen recent polls. In fact, today, just before we started this hearing, Turkish support for the government's Syrian and Iraq policy has plummeted, for the first time under 50 percent. This used to be a 70 percent, 76 percent support in 2011. Now it is 41 percent support for government Syria policy.

Mr. KEATING. I take it in your answer that you thought there was some type of aid that was there at least before. Has that ceased?

Mr. CAGAPTAY. I would not call it aid, Congressman. I think it was a policy of basically anticipating that whoever went in would be cleaned out eventually. I think Turkey is now basically coming to grips with the realization that this is a long term problem and it will work closer with U.S. and European allies.

Mr. KEATING. Dr. Kanat, do you want to comment on that?

Mr. KANAT. I agree with some of Dr. Cagaptay's statements about this. Turkey and Syria have more than a 500-mile border without any geographical terrain. So it is very difficult to control the border. And then Turkish-Syrian relations were extremely bad in the 1990s. There was a huge land mine that basically had a post—a military post and everything. But since the improvement of the relations and rapprochement, Turkey removed this and Turkey and Syria had good relations and no visa requirements; it was basically an open border.

Now after the Arab Spring and the starting of the Assad regime's killing of its own people, there is this major problem. There is this border, a huge border—500-mile border—and it is very difficult to control who is entering and who is not in those circumstances. Turkey and United States launch a, actually, initiative, antiterrorism initiative, and Turkey and both countries contributed to this $500 million last year. And about the ISIS there is, starting from the emergence of this trend Turkey basically indicated several times that ISIS may be a major threat not only for Turkey but for the region as a whole.

Mr. KEATING. In the remaining seconds, if I could, I would just like to ask Mr. Tasci. Business community, when they are hearing these things, when they are hearing about issues about separation of powers, rule of law issues and the closure of communications like YouTube, can you just comment what the conversation is among the business communities? And you can touch on the Soma mining disaster as well. What is the chatter in the business communities? Just briefly, so it doesn't go too much longer over time.

Mr. TASCI. What is going on in Turkey is a big concern for many business people as well. For example, I will give a couple of things which are in my prepared statement as well. TUSIAD chairman, for example, one of our competitors, let us say, business association chairman said, we need rule of law. I mean he made a comment about rule of law and the importance of rule of law for international investors. And the response was he is a traitor, I mean he got the reaction in a public mass that traitors. And after 3 or 4 months he had very unusual things happening and he resigned because of his own business interests. And now they have a new chairman which had his first meeting with the prime minister and the other cabinet members as well.

And I am sure he is here as well, American-Turkish Council chairman and CEO, James Holmes, is one of the leading businessperson or one of the leading individual who represents the business community in United States is the chair of ATC. His institution is blacklisted, and his conference, which they held last June was the 33rd of that conference and the Turkish Government blocked it and they didn't come to the event and he signed his resignation because of that one.

So I mean this kind of treatment is not unique to one institution or another but rather for everyone. You have to comply. You have to be silent or you have to face the consequences.

Mr. KEATING. Thank you. I think you have given us a flavor. We did ask other business groups if they were interested in this hearing. And I want to thank you for being here. Because I think much of the progress that Turkey will have and we will have together with Turkey will be grounded on economic activities, and certainly some of the concerns you raised are concerns that may affect that progress. Thank you, I yield back.

Mr. ROHRABACHER. And as the Chair noted in the opening statement, quite often economic progress can be short circuited and cut off if the political system does not match the progress going on in the economic system.

Mr. Sires?

Mr. SIRES. Thank you, Mr. Chairman, for holding this hearing. But I find Turkey almost like an enigma. A few years ago they were poised to be one of the leading countries in the country that were an example. Now I see all these pivoting back, more repressive, less democracy concerns. I was just wondering if you see this because of the region they are in and there are concerns all around them, or is there an excuse that they are using to pivot away from what I think was a democratic way?

Mr. SCHENKKAN. Thank you, Congressman. I think that Turkey has obviously suffered through a very difficult history of coups, of illiberalism of a single party period at the founding of the country. The democratic tradition in Turkey has been weak even though it was a multiparty system after World War II.

So you have this long history leading up to the rise of the AK Party that the party came within that context. And I don't think the party has escaped that context, and perhaps we shouldn't be as surprised as we feel we are. But what we are seeing is the AK Party after this period that Dr. Cagaptay mentioned, in the early 2000s when the EU accession process was more active, when the AK Party was more actively courting a liberal democratic trend for several years, I would say at least going back to 2007, we have seen the party led by the prime minister reinstituting many of the habits, reenacting many of the habits of the illiberal state.

And because the mechanisms of the illiberal state are still there in the judiciary, in the police forces, to a certain degree in the culture that is finding fertile ground and it is something that can be enacted and it is something that is developing.

Mr. SIRES. Would you like to respond?

Mr. CAGAPTAY. Thank you, Congressman. I think Turkey is a democracy. It remains a democracy. It has free and fair elections.

Mr. SIRES. But it is pivoting away.

Mr. CAGAPTAY. Governments, I agree with you. Governments can be voted out. I think the trend we are seeing is not that it is undemocratic, it has a democratically elected government which does rule in an authoritarian fashion. And I think that suggests a consolidation of two branches of government in one hand, executive and legislative, and if Prime Minister Erdogan is elected as President he will also appoint judges to the high courts also holding power over judiciary. But Turkey does remain a democracy. It has robust democratic institutions and the governments are voted in and out democratically.

Mr. SIRES. They also in my eyes are very sensitive to anything in terms of the Armenian genocide or the recent, that we did in the committee—return of the properties, the churches and everything else. I had a senior moment, I guess. I should say that, right?

But I mean, how can I say this? I don't know. I just see it as turning away from all the good things that they have done. I mean I even see, I know we are not supposed to bring up the Cyprus issue, but they act like thugs. Even when you go and vote here you feel like you are voting with the Turkish order we had on any of those issues. I mean if you are going to be a country of 75 million people and you are going to be a world player, you have got a great history, I mean you have to be more understanding that you can't be a thug.

And I just feel that is the way they behave in many ways, and I don't know whether that is due to the growing pains or it is just in the culture. Maybe it is in their history. But if you want to be a player, you want to be part of the European Union, you have other ways of dealing with many of the issues that they seem to go war.

Mr. CAGAPTAY. As an historian, if I could respond to your dilemma, I follow the reaction to the passage of the resolution in Turkish media, in Turkish, and I think the reaction was not so much anger at the passing of the resolution but the fact that Turkey has made some progress in restoring, for example, property belonging to synagogue and church foundations after passing a law in 2011. It hasn't restored all property. It has restored property totaling about $1 billion in value.

Mr. SIRES. I get all that.

Mr. CAGAPTAY. Yes, yes.

Mr. SIRES. I understand all that. But if you are going to say something negative about a country——

Mr. CAGAPTAY. Right.

Mr. SIRES [continuing]. Look at what can say about the United States. I mean we are like the evil empire. Everybody criticizes no matter what we do. But if you want to be a role player in this country, want to be in this world, you have 75 million people with all this history, I just find that for me perplexing. And maybe I just don't know enough about the history and I am now not being accurate. Thank you, Chairman.

Mr. ROHRABACHER. Thank you. And Mr. Connolly?

Mr. CONNOLLY. I thank the chairman and I thank my friend the ranking member as well for allowing me to participate. Well, first of all, I would say to my dear friend Mr. Sires, I am not sure much is achieved by referring to the Turkish Government, a NATO ally that has been there by our side for the entirety of the Cold War and since, as a thug. I just don't think that is helpful. I also think it is not true to history. And I——

Mr. SIRES. I am not setting policies.

Mr. CONNOLLY. I know. I know. And I would just say with respect to Cyprus, actually there is a lot of good news coming out of Cyprus recently, finally, and we want to encourage that. And we want to be careful about that because the two sides are talking and there is actually movement and some sense of hope. And I would hope Congress would encourage that.

I will also say while I certainly appreciate this hearing, I don't know how often we have a hearing on a fellow European country and member of NATO to investigate how they are doing in their internal political process. And I might even have some candidates for us to consider if we are going to extend the list. Turkey is a work in progress as a democracy, so are we. And I would never justify the crackdown on the press, freedom of religion, freedom of expression, but imperfect is not the same as being hopeless and retrograde and autocratic and authoritarian and oppressive.

And one of the concerns I have, quite frankly, in our full committee is sometimes that gets lost in our rhetoric and even in our actions. And we want to encourage Turkish democracy. We want to encourage a secular Muslim society in Turkey. We want to encourage Turkish membership in the EU. We need to get over biases and historical problems. Turkey has to come to acknowledgment with some of its past, as my friend from New Jersey has indicated, but so do others. And we need to deal with the Turkey of here and now, not of the Turkey of 100 years ago or 200 years ago or 500 years ago for that matter. Some of us are still hung up on Constantinople. But we have to deal with what we are dealing with here and now.

And so none of that is to excuse behavior that looks like, to your point Mr. Sires, a regression. And maybe it is structural and maybe it is personal and maybe it is both. We have got a government that has been in power for quite some time and frankly doesn't have much political opposition that is viable. That is always a dangerous situation for any democracy because we get complacent, we get arrogant and the like.

So let me ask starting with you, Mr. Tasci, from the business community's point of view. Do you believe that the Erdogan government is regressing? That in fact we are risking democratization, democratic institutions with some sense of arrogance of purpose with this current government?

Mr. TASCI. So good question, Mr. Congressman. Hard to answer, but I will try to be as precise as possible. I am talking about one person and the problems with one person does not necessarily mean the problem is the problem of everyone in that sector or everyone who supported that party or other kind of people. And you may be having problems on one side like the one that I mentioned about the Gulen movement and other kind of things, but you may have very progressive and very good policymakers when people are on your side.

So I mean that is the kind of different approach compared to like Chinese type or like Korean type or different types of countries. I mean definitely Turkey is a democracy. Turkey may be a liberal democracy or maybe it is like majoritarian democracy. You may call it any way you can. But we have free elections. Is it fair? Questionable. Does the government use its power to enhance and improve their own networks and success? I think there may be some legitimacy on that. But in general it is going to be very hard to say it is not——

Mr. CONNOLLY. If I may, Mr. Chairman, could I ask Mr. Schenkkan if he wants to respond to that as well?

Mr. SCHENKKAN. Yes, thank you. Yes, there is regression under-way. This is being documented by Freedom House. It is being docu-mented by other human rights organizations, by journalists on the ground, by international journalists. This is a major subject of dis-cussion for everyone who is following Turkey closely. We are seeing the regression in all areas of fundamental freedoms. We are seeing it in freedom of expression. We are seeing it in freedom of associa-tion. We are seeing it in freedom of assembly.

And I want to stress that just to anticipate the counter argument that I am sure the congressmen have heard elsewhere that this is nothing compared to what it was like in the 1990s or in the 1980s under military rule or during the dirty wars. That is true. That doesn't mean that that is the standard for Turkey. Turkey is, as we have said repeatedly, an EU member candidate country. It is also a signatory to the European Convention on Human Rights which is legally binding. There are a whole host of ways in which Turkey's aspirations and the standard to which Turkey holds itself are much higher.

Mr. CONNOLLY. Thank you.

Mr. CAGAPTAY. Congressman, if I may? I agree with you, Con-gressman, that what we see in Turkey is a real progress and that should be recognized primarily because the country has come a long way especially on the economic sphere and that is significant. Countries cannot be transformed politically unless they are trans-formed economically first. So Turkey has done the first part of this tough task. It has become a majority middle class society and that is a legacy of Prime Minister Erdogan.

If, as my colleague here, Dr. Kanat, says, Prime Minister Erdogan does commit himself to drafting a liberal democratic Con-stitution for the country, he will also go down in history as the per-son who has transformed the country politically. He has not done that so far. And I think given his political record, it is possible to expect that that political transformation is probably not going to come from within the governing party but from the liberal opposi-tion that has been building in Turkey in the last decade primarily because of the AKP's successful economic policies, which have pro-duced a majority middle class society which now demands respect for individual liberties, freedoms of expression, media, association and assembly. This was the tone of the Gezi Park movement and I think it is going to stay around in Turkish politics.

So we could conclude that Prime Minister Erdogan has trans-formed Turkey economically, but it is the liberals—and I am using the word ''liberal'' here not in the American sense but in the Euro-pean sense. It is the liberals who are committed to democracy who will transform Turkey politically.

Mr. KANAT. Thank you. I think part of this discussion is about what authoritarianism is, as Prime Minister Erdogan is winning elections and becoming the predominant leader in Turkey. And we have to understand that not all predominant leaders are prone to authoritarianism, not always. And when you see the reform pack-ages, especially regarding the Kurdish question, the historic proc-ess that we are having right now and the condolences that offered for the Armenians, this couldn't be happening with a predominant leader.

And we have to understand that democratization is a moving target, and I totally understand that for some in Turkey the current level of democratization may not be enough and comparing constantly with the 1990s or the previous decades may not be a good way to understand this. So I think it is a moving target and it is a learning process at the same time.

But Prime Minister Erdogan and the AK Party government, from the reform processes that they are in right now and from their determination to write a civilian and pluralistic Constitution, gave the signal that especially the period after the elections would be a new democratic process.

Mr. CONNOLLY. You have been most generous. Thank you, Mr. Chairman.

Mr. ROHRABACHER. Actually it is the Chairman's policy that people have a chance to answer the questions and then if there is a discussion that is getting to an important point that we don't put the 5-minute rule into effect in a way to cut off some people from getting down to some truths that we are looking for. With that said, Mr. Lowenthal, I know, will take about 20 minutes now.

Mr. LOWENTHAL. Thank you for offering me ½ hour to speak.

Mr. KEATING. We want you to take 5 minutes.

Mr. LOWENTHAL. It is okay. May be an improvement.

I don't know what question, I want to kind of frame it in my concerns. About 6 years ago when I was a member of the California State Legislature we took a visit, some of the leadership in the legislature, to Turkey and it was a time of great excitement. It was a time of, it was, I think, the second term of the AKP party. We met with leadership in the Justice and Development Party not with Mr. Erdogan but with others just below. And it was a time of where there was a great change there.

At that point as I understood, Turkey had had a history of every 20 years or so a military coup, and the party was trying to reduce the role of the military at the time. He was in a major battle with the generals to reduce their power. He was also, I remember at that time when I was there, there were great newspaper stories about the fight between the justice system and his wanting to replace many of the justices because of some of the tremendous corruption that had taken place historically. There was greater freedom. There was discussion on the streets. We met with women's groups in terms of the role of women. And so it was a time of great hope and aspiration. We spent time with families. We didn't stay in hotels, we spent with families as we went across the country visiting schools.

And synonymous with this and with this tremendous support was a greater amount of religious toleration. And we kept meeting with people who were very much pro-AKP party and also some of the people who were in the Gulen movement who were very synonymous and very similar and really talked about how it was not a threat. Unfortunately while this is happening, I have been hearing more and more about the threat to religious freedoms that are taking place. That a movement that was seen as not anti, not really anti or pro-government, was now, was really talking about the role of education, the role of people, the role was now beginning more and more to be perceived as threatening.

And so my question is, is this so? Is this really what is going on? I am sure you have talked about it. And I realize that over time governments change. It has now been almost, what, the AKP was, which I believe before 2002 was not even a major party. It was really, and so it has been only now 14 years as a party, but it has been a party that has been in power for 14 years.

So I am really concerned about what the future holds and whether this apparent, is what I heard before, slide away from democracy, slightly, maybe not totally, but some of this movement and this lack of religious tolerance is really so, and what role can we play in both supporting Turkey and also supporting a movement toward democracy?

Yes?

Ms. PRODROMOU. I think that your observations are correct that there has been backsliding and also there are some danger signals when it comes to religious tolerance. I think it is important for us to understand that when we speak about secularism in Turkey and Turkey as a secular democracy, Turkey secularism has in no way meant freedom of religion from the state. The Turkish model of secularism has been promised on the absolute state control over religion in civil society. And I think that is a very different understanding of secularism and therefore leads to very different kinds of consequences with religious——

Mr. LOWENTHAL. Many of these schools that we visited were set up by people who followed the leadership of Gulen. Has that been seen as a threat that now they are educating children in a different way? I just wonder if the threat is that people, although, and my impression was Gulen, and this movement when we talked to it was not anti the government at all, but yet it was pro-education, pro-parental involvement in the schools. Tremendous change in how the schools—is this being seen as a threat to Turkish or centralized control over both education or religion?

Ms. PRODROMOU. The initial collaboration and cooperation between the Gulenist movement and civil society and the AKP party has been well documented. And I think that——

Mr. LOWENTHAL. And it was that you could feel it when you were in the country.

Ms. PRODROMOU. And the expansion and tolerance for Islam in the public sphere for Turkey's Muslim population has been significant. And I think that is a function, initially, of the cooperation between the AKP and the Gulenist movement. That kind of expansion, however, and the public presence of the Sunni majority population has not been matched by an equal expansion and tolerance for, for example, the 20 percent Alawite population in Turkey, and it certainly hasn't been matched by increased tolerance for non-Muslim minorities in Turkey.

And I think another piece of this discussion that needs to be addressed is the rising anti-Semitism that we have witnessed in Turkey over the last decade, in particular the kinds of public statements by even this warning by Prime Minister Erdogan regarding the interest rate lobby, the Jewish lobby, et cetera that has led to, I think, a generalized societal intolerance for non-Muslim minorities in Turkey including the Jewish community.

Circling back though to the Galenist-AKP relationship, again I think that the initial globalization that allowed for greater public presence for Islam in Turkey was driven by the Galenist movement, but with the cleavage now between the current government and that movement I think we are beginning to see a backlash.

Mr. SCHENKKAN. Congressman?

Mr. ROHRABACHER. Very quickly.

Mr. SCHENKKAN. Yes, a short comment on that. I think the greatest achievement of the AKP in democratization was loosening the grip on identity on who could be a Turk, who could legitimately be a Turkish citizen. As my colleague said though that was done primarily for the purposes of liberating people to be conservative Muslims in public. It did have an effect though across society, and Turkish identity now is much more flexible and much more open and that is a very positive development.

The biggest question now in this regard is will, under President Erdogan will a new unitary identity start to be established and start to be enforced? And that is probably the most frightening consequence that could come out of the consolidation of power.

Mr. ROHRABACHER. Let us quickly——

Mr. CAGAPTAY. Thank you. On the issue of the rights of, and religious freedoms with members in communities, as someone who has often gone on the record to criticize the government's record on liberties I have to disagree with my copanelist, Dr. Prodromou, with that. The government has actually done well on the religious rights of the non-Muslim communities and improved significantly.

I have visited this Greek Orthodox Sumela Monastery, Armenian Aghtamar Church in the last years. They were both restored with government funds, public money. Public money has been spent now to pay for utility bills of churches and synagogues, a practice that the government has been doing for a very long time for mosques. That is equality if that could be construed as such.

On the broader picture, Congressman, on your question of Turkey's direction on religion and state, I think there are, broadly speaking, two practices of organizing the relation between religion and politics. One is the European system which is freedom from religion in education and politics, and the other one is the American system which is freedom of religion in education and politics. Turks for a long time practiced the first under Kemalism. Because they were Europeans this was laïcité. This is how the Europeans do it.

They have switched to the second model, the American model, from religion to freedom of religion, education and politics. I think Turkey needs both to move forward because it is a country that has Muslims and non-Muslims. It has shades of Islam. It has shades of practice or the lack thereof. And to accommodate this diversity of Islam as well as non-Islam and faith and non-faith and practice and non-faith practice, Turkey needs to be a country that provides for not just freedom for religion, education and politics, which is what it does now, but also freedom from religion, education and politics. These two, I think, will be the way to move Turkey forward. Thank you.

Mr. KANAT. I want to add a couple things to the religious freedom side. The Sumela Monastery and Aghtamar Church was renovated and restored, and in the Sumela Monastery, actually, after

100 years, the first religious services took place in 2012. And same in 2013, in the Aghtamar Church, after 88 years, the first religious services are taking place. So there is improvement in the rights of the non-Muslim community in Turkey.

And one more thing I want to add about press freedom. You have to understand that when we are discussing press freedom in Turkey and censorship, there is a plurality of newspapers in Turkey. Actually, there are around 40 newspapers in Turkey with a total circulation of 5 million. And 65 percent—60 percent—of these newspapers are anti-government and you can see all kinds of anti-government news in these newspapers. The problem is that none of the newspapers have pluralism within them so they become almost homogenous entities, and fighting journalists, I think, would take place in anti-government newspapers as well. For example, if you write a pro-government column in one of the newspapers—anti-government newspapers—you would probably lose your job immediately. And because of that, as I was mentioning, there is a structural—deep structural—problem to understand press freedom in Turkey and to provide any kind of solution for this problem. Thank you.

Mr. ROHRABACHER. Thank you. And we have one last comment, but let us just note there are journalists here who lose their job because they are not towing the line of whoever management is in charge as well. Do you want to make one comment on that and then we will go there?

Mr. SCHENKKAN. Thank you. If I may, to respond on the press freedom issue as it is a special focus. I think there is somewhat of a simplistic understanding sometimes of what it means to not have freedom of expression in a repressive environment. It is not that one makes a statement and then a piano falls on you or trap door opens and you disappear through the floor.

What happens in Turkey, what happens often, what happens dozens if not hundreds of times is that people are fired for speaking out, for criticizing the government. They are fired through direct government intervention. Through direct intervention from government officials with newspaper and media owners. We know that this happens. This has been confirmed. They are also sued. They face criminal and civil defamation suits. They are even sent to jail for certain kinds of reporting.

Mr. ROHRABACHER. That is a very significant point to make in reference to the point that was made. Finally, the last——

Mr. TASCI. One small thing I would like to add, as you asked what happened suddenly with this Gulen movement and AK Party thing, I would like to say one thing about it. I think you are right that there was a heavy support and religious movements or religious ideologies from all sects in Turkey saw by AK Party as their own garden. And especially after 2011 elections when they had that vast majority, 49 percent of election victory right after the referendum. They feel like it is time to control the religious area as well, but the movement was independent as well.

So the movement stays independent, becomes independent which makes the government a little bit troublesome. As force, a civil society force, which is very organized, they may lose in several fronts of the community, educational institutions, dialogue centers, et cetera, but they cannot be controlled. You cannot tell them what to do.

So the monopolization of this religious domain also become an important factor for this separation. For example, other movements have the similar problems. New movements, for example, have their own books and now the government is publicizing that book's publication. So I mean they don't have the right to publish their own books that they wrote, but the government institutions have to publish it and it is going to give the books to them. So controlling everything is the main sense and is the main reason I can say.

Mr. ROHRABACHER. All right. The Chair will now ask the ranking member if he would like to have 2 minutes to summarize his views on the hearing today, and then I will make a 2-minute summary as well and that will be it.

Mr. KEATING. Thank you, Mr. Chairman. Even our own members have asked why are we having hearings, why Turkey, why not other countries? We touched upon the fact that over the last short period of time Turkey has become much more influential in the world. And Turkey, I believe, has the opportunity to become even more influential in the world.

So their policies now that they are in this position and have the potential to move further, their policies now go beyond their borders more than they did before and they have influenced beyond their own borders more than before including the United States. Turkey is our strategic partner and we want to keep it that way. The U.S. has an interest in Turkey's democracy becoming stronger. The U.S. has an interest in Turkey's economy becoming stronger, and we should do whatever we can to help keep that progress moving forward and not backwards.

And that is something that I think most of us and I think all of us can agree upon as we look at this hearing. There is a lot at stake. There is a lot of progress. There is a lot that can be done to help the region and the world. And we are very attentive to Turkey and we are very attentive to things that aren't moving in a direction where our own interests, Turkey's interests, in fact, European interests and world interests can all be benefited by that. I yield back.

Mr. ROHRABACHER. I would like to thank our witnesses. I hope that you were able to make the points that you needed to make and that we got into some areas of discussion that I think are important. That is the purpose of these congressional hearings, is not necessarily to come to the ultimate conclusion but instead to make sure that people are discussing issues of significance. And you have given us a lot of food for thought today so I appreciate all of you for testifying.

Let me just note that just from the chairman's perspective, some cultures can't accept criticism very well. One of the great attributes of Americans is that we generally can take criticism. In fact, when people are saying you are doing this wrong or you are doing that wrong, we usually think of it as a good suggestion. Let us go take a look at it and maybe we can correct it.

And over the years we have certainly had our share of maladies and sins that we committed against our own people, and with the open system, and we didn't always have a free press here. And we had a freer press than in other places of the world, but we did have people who are in various parts of our country faced physical retaliation if they said something bad about the Ku Klux Klan for a long time.

But we basically, our country now that when people criticize us we are able to accept that. I don't think that the Turkish culture is the same as the American culture in this regard. And that is why when people want to talk about what happened in the Armenian genocide, the Turkish people then think it is a personal attack on them even though this is something that happened about 100 years ago.

And certainly if someone started going through the sins that we committed against the American Indians or against Black Americans 75 years ago, we wouldn't probably have the same, how do you say, sensitivity to it. We would just say, well, we have tried our best and if there is still some remnants around we are going to make it better even more so.

So we have to understand that about Turkey. That is part of their culture. Today our intent was not just to offer criticisms but to understand what is going on and to perhaps communicate with our friends, and all the Turkish people are our friends. That we have got some concerns that over the last 10 years we were very joyful that things seemed to be going in the right direction and now there is some indications that it might not be going in the right direction.

And that is not to say that is worse off than it was under the Ataturk regimes that took place for so long, but that there are reasons there are trim lines. I will just say this that when, under Ataturk and that regime, young women in the universities were not permitted to wear head scarves. And some of my friends, when they permitted women to wear head scarves at the university, came to me and said how horrible it is to see this radical Islamic regime there, they are allowing women to wear head scarves. No, it is when women are mandated to wear head scarves that the line is crossed and that we should be concerned.

So there are some areas of concern that we should have about freedom of press and making sure that people who demonstrate are not incarcerated, et cetera. But we always have to put this in perspective and try of what is going on in other countries but also in how it relates to our basic principles as a people. And again, the last point is we should not forget that the Turks have stood with us for so long and through so many trials during the Cold War, we need to keep them as our friends and we need to offer our criticisms not as criticisms but as suggestions of how they can improve things and get things on the right track. With that said this hearing is adjourned.

[Whereupon, at 4:40 p.m., the subcommittee was adjourned.]

APPENDIX

———

MATERIAL SUBMITTED FOR THE RECORD

SUBCOMMITTEE HEARING NOTICE
COMMITTEE ON FOREIGN AFFAIRS
U.S. HOUSE OF REPRESENTATIVES
WASHINGTON, DC 20515-6128

Subcommittee on Europe, Eurasia, and Emerging Threats
Dana Rohrabacher (R-CA), Chairman

July 11, 2014

TO: MEMBERS OF THE COMMITTEE ON FOREIGN AFFAIRS

You are respectfully requested to attend an OPEN hearing of the Committee on Foreign Affairs, to be held by the Subcommittee on Europe, Eurasia, and Emerging Threats in Room 2200 of the Rayburn House Office Building (and available live on the Committee website at http://www.ForeignAffairs.house.gov):

DATE: Tuesday, July 15, 2014

TIME: 2:00 p.m.

SUBJECT: The Future of Turkish Democracy

WITNESSES: Mr. Nate Schenkkan
                   Program Officer
                   Eurasia Programs
                   Freedom House

                   Elizabeth H. Prodromou, Ph.D.
                   Visiting Associate Professor of Conflict Resolution
                   The Fletcher School of Law and Diplomacy
                   Tufts University

                   Soner Cagaptay, Ph.D.
                   Beyer Family Fellow and Director
                   Turkish Research Program
                   The Washington Institute for Near East Policy

                   Kilic Kanat, Ph.D.
                   Non-Resident Scholar
                   Foundation for Political, Economic, and Social Research (SETA)

                   Mr. Hakan Tasci
                   Executive Director
                   Tuskon-US

By Direction of the Chairman

The Committee on Foreign Affairs seeks to make its facilities accessible to persons with disabilities. If you are in need of special accommodations, please call 202/225-5021 at least four business days in advance of the event, whenever practicable. Questions with regard to special accommodations in general (including availability of Committee materials in alternative formats and assistive listening devices) may be directed to the Committee.

COMMITTEE ON FOREIGN AFFAIRS

MINUTES OF SUBCOMMITTEE ON _____ *Europe, Eurasia and Emerging Threats* _____ HEARING

Day ___*Tuesday*___ Date ___*July 15, 2014*___ Room ___*2200*___

Starting Time ___*2:03pm*___ Ending Time ___*4:50pm*___

Recesses [*2:19*] (*3:09* to ___) (___ to ___) (___ to ___) (___ to ___) (___ to ___) (___ to ___)

Presiding Member(s)

Rep. Rohrabacher

Check all of the following that apply:

Open Session ☐   Electronically Recorded (taped) ☑
Executive (closed) Session ☐   Stenographic Record ☐
Televised ☐

TITLE OF HEARING:

The Future of Turkish Democracy

SUBCOMMITTEE MEMBERS PRESENT:

Rep. Keating, Rep. Duncan, Rep. Sires, Rep. Holding

NON-SUBCOMMITTEE MEMBERS PRESENT: *(Mark with an * if they are not members of full committee.)*

Rep. Royce, Rep. Connolly

HEARING WITNESSES: Same as meeting notice attached? Yes ☑ No ☐
(If "no", please list below and include title, agency, department, or organization.)

STATEMENTS FOR THE RECORD: *(List any statements submitted for the record.)*

Rep. Keating

TIME SCHEDULED TO RECONVENE _____
or
TIME ADJOURNED ___*4:50pm*___

_____
Subcommittee Staff Director

Congressman George Holding
Statement for the Record
EE&ET Subcommittee Hearing on 'The Future of Turkish Democracy'

Mr. Chairman, our bilateral relationship with Turkey is one that is rooted in mutual cooperation and shared values. It is also a relationship that has plenty of room for growth and enhanced ties. Turkey is a NATO ally which has strategic significance for not only the United States but for our other allies as well. Further, Turkey's geographic location positions them well to serve as a major transit corridor for trade and energy that is vitally important for our European allies.

Last year, I was in Istanbul as the Gezi Park Protests began. Since then, we have seen a string of troubling news stories ranging from the shutdown of Twitter and YouTube, to high-level corruption allegations, to the closure of schools, to the reports of the judiciary and press being restricted. Taken either by themselves or as a whole, they are certainly a reason to pause and ask about the current course on which Turkey is headed. Turkey has a proud legacy of liberalization in the 20th Century so it is hard not to see these recent developments as a step backwards.

But as we in Congress take up legislation or hold hearings with regards to Turkey, we would be well-served to also be cognizant of Turkey's current security and refugee situation – something I feel is often appreciated but not fully brought into the discussion. While their current situation should considered, it in no way excuses the shutdown of Twitter or YouTube or any of the other troubling reports that cast a shadow on Turkey's democratic history.

With the economic growth Turkey has experienced combined with their European Union aspirations comes certain expectations. This is why we ask questions about the trajectory of Turkey's democracy that has been for many years has been a model in their neck of the woods.

Mr. Chairman, Turkey is preparing for a presidential election next month followed by Grand National Assembly elections next summer. Over the last few years, talk of changing Turkey's Constitution to provide the President with significantly increased powers and authorities has been a concern for many. The actions – or inaction – taken over the next year by Turkish politicians with regards to increasing Presidential power will speak volumes as to the future of Turkish democracy.

It is certainly my hope – and I am sure the hope of everyone on our Subcommittee – that Turkey alters their current course and regains their footing as a beacon of democracy in a part of the world where freedoms such as open and fair elections, religion, an independent judiciary, and free press are increasingly fading away. I certainly believe this can be achieved and firmly believe that this is the desire of the Turkish people.

Thank you Mr. Chairman.

Statement for the Record
Submitted by Mr. Connolly of Virginia

I thank the distinguished Chairman for allowing me to participate today and for calling this hearing to examine how the House Committee on Foreign Affairs can play a constructive role in promoting democracy in Turkey. Turkey is a close ally of the United States and has remained a trusted member of NATO for over 60 years. Turkish democracy remains a work in progress, and so long as guidance is required, it is incumbent upon the United States and our allies to engage Turkey on a basis that is consistent with a relationship of mutual assistance. We neglect this relationship at our own peril. Turkey is in proximity to several global flashpoints and is strategically valuable to our capability to respond to regional crises. A robust future for Turkish democracy is in the best interest of the Turkish people, American-Turkish relations, and American national security.

The Republic of Turkey was founded in 1923. At the time, there were fewer than 30 democracies in the world. Today, there are over 100. We have learned from the global proliferation of democracy that it is through encouragement and assistance from the U.S. that countries around the world establish and grow democracies. As countries have found their way, they have discovered that democratic transitions are often beset with deviations. They are dynamic, they experience setbacks at times, and democracies often take generations to mature to the point of stability. Several military coups and a period of single-party rule have demonstrated that Turkish democracy is no exception to the rule of nonlinear democratic development.

A case study on the value of engaging and incentivizing Turkish democracy has been Turkey's accession to the European Union. Turkey is a promising candidate country for European Union (EU) membership. However, handwringing in Europe has dragged the formal accession process into its eighth year, undermining the bulwarks of democratic reform and allowing Turkish Prime Minister Recep Tayyip Erdogan to demonstrate that he is capable of the occasional clumsy and tone-deaf power-grab.

The EU exists because institutions matter. Institutions promote shared values and achieve common goals. The EU accession process fortifies institutions within candidate countries and aligns them with the democracies of Europe. The accession process in Turkey precipitated structural improvements to the domestic economy and forced the issue of governance reform in Ankara, but the EU has been consistently slow to open new chapters of the *acquis communautaire* and engage Turkish institutions on the implementation of European law. Progress must be made on Cyprus, but no single issue should be allowed to obscure the wider goal or serve as justification for prejudging the outcome of the reform process.

Accession stalled long before Gezi Park, and Mr. Erdogan has filled the vacuum created by idle negotiations with his own brand of reform. Most recently, Prime Minister Erdogan has threatened the independence of the judiciary, stifled freedom of expression, and undermined corruption investigations. Leaders of the business community have urged political moderation and pleaded for a renewed focus on a national economy that currently boasts the 6th largest trading relationship with the EU.

As we consider the future of Turkish democracy, I hope we do so in context of our strategic relationship with Turkey on issues of regional security. The crisis we are witnessing in Iraq could very well require that Turkey once again play a strategic role in partnering with the U.S. to preserve regional stability. Turkey has already played a vital and unheralded role responding to another crisis in the region by accommodating over 1 million refugees fleeing the violence in Syria. Turkey also maintains a watchful eye on Russia's destabilization of Ukraine across the Black Sea and the nuclear ambitions of its neighbor Iran. Turkey has an important role to play on behalf of Western interests in the greater Middle East as the only Muslim-majority country in the world with a secular democracy. It is a vital strategic partner as a NATO ally and served as a non-permanent member of the United Nations Security Council. Isolating Turkey or allowing Turkey to isolate itself serves no end, certainly not that of regional stability and security.

As the co-chair of the Congressional Study Group on Turkey and the co-chair of the Congressional Caucus on Turkey and Turkish-Americans, I thank my colleagues and our witnesses for sharing my interest in the important matter of Turkish democracy. If we are sincere about the cause of democratic transition around the globe, certainly we will find that promoting Turkish democracy in a way that is inclusive and constructive is within our reach.